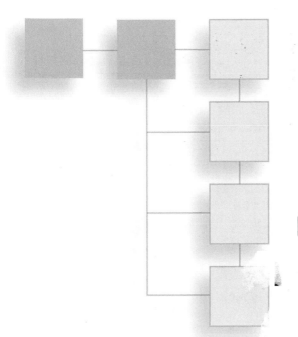

GAME CREATION

return

JASON DARBY

Course Technology PTR

A part of Cengage Learning

 COURSE TECHNOLOGY
CENGAGE Learning™

Australia • Brazil • Japan • Korea • Mexico • Singapore • Spain • United Kingdom • United States

COURSE TECHNOLOGY
CENGAGE Learning™

Game Creation for Teens
Jason Darby

Publisher and General Manager, Course Technology PTR: Stacy L. Hiquet

Associate Director of Marketing: Sarah Panella

Manager of Editorial Services: Heather Talbot

Marketing Manager: Jordan Casey

Acquisitions Editor: Heather Hurley

Project and Copy Editor: Marta Justak

Technical Reviewer: Danny Vink

Teen Reviewer: Hannah Wittig

PTR Editorial Services Coordinator: Erin Johnson

Interior Layout Tech: ICC Macmillan Inc.

Cover Designer: Mike Tanamachi

CD-ROM Producer: Brandon Penticuff

Indexer: Sharon Shock

Proofreader: Cathleen Small

For product information and technology assistance, contact us at **Cengage Learning Customer & Sales Support, 1-800-354-9706**

For permission to use material from this text or product, submit all requests online at **cengage.com/permissions**
Further permissions questions can be emailed to
permissionrequest@cengage.com

Games Factory 2 is copyright of Clickteam.com. Future Tennis, Quick Draw, and Last Pursuit are copyright of Castle Software Ltd and 3dlight-studio.com. Stronghold and CivCity Rome are copyright of FireFly Studios. Forza 2 Motor Sport, Microsoft® Flight Simulator X, Halo® 2, and Fable are all copyright of Microsoft. All other trademarks are the property of their respective owners.

Library of Congress Control Number: 2008920095

ISBN-13: 978-1-59863-500-3

ISBN-10: 1-59863-500-X

Course Technology
25 Thomson Place
Boston, MA 02210
USA

Cengage Learning is a leading provider of customized learning solutions with office locations around the globe, including Singapore, the United Kingdom, Australia, Mexico, Brazil, and Japan. Locate your local office at: **international.cengage.com/region**

Cengage Learning products are represented in Canada by Nelson Education, Ltd.

For your lifelong learning solutions, visit **courseptr.com**

Visit our corporate Website at **cengage.com**

Printed in the United States of America
1 2 3 4 5 6 7 11 10 09 08

*To my wonderful family, Alicia, Jared, Kimberley,
and Lucas, for all their support.*

ACKNOWLEDGMENTS

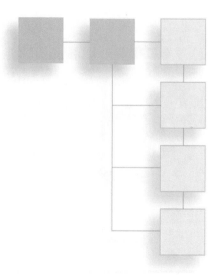

I would like to thank a number of people who have helped me and have been involved in the creation of the book, which without their help, this book would not have been made.

To my wife Alicia, my children, Jared, Kimberley, and Lucas, who have supported me through this project.

To Raymond of www.3dlight-studio.com, who created some amazing graphics and games for the book. Without his help, I would have taken a lot longer to complete the book.

To my good friends, Yves Lamoureux, Francois Lionet. and Jeff Vance, who provided me with help and support to ensure the book was as complete as it could be.

To the professional and very friendly staff at Course PTR, who again have provided excellent support throughout the whole process.

About the Author

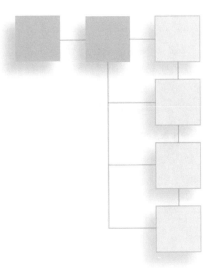

Jason Darby has been working in the IT industry for the past decade writing user and systems documentation for users with little or no knowledge of the programs they were using. For a number of years, he has been director of his own company, Castle Software Ltd., working in the games and application creation market where he has been making games, applications, and CD demos. Jason is the author of *Make Amazing Games in Minutes, Power Users Guide to Windows Development,* and *Awesome Game Creation, Third Edition,* which were published by Charles River Media, a part of Cengage Learning.

CONTENTS

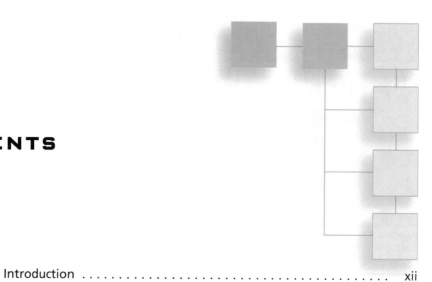

INTRODUCTION

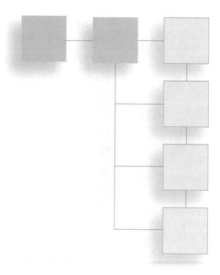

Welcome to the book *Game Creation for Teens*. This book is aimed at anyone who wants to make exciting and fun games for Windows. You'll learn how to make a number of games in a drag-and-drop game creation system that requires no programming knowledge. By the end of the book, you will know how to make three amazing and exciting games and be ready to make your own.

Audience

If you've purchased this book or are reading it in a bookstore, then we can assume you're interested in making computer games. You may be in school or college at the moment and want to make a fun game for your friends and family, create a game that you've always wanted to do, or just want a bit of fun.

Aim of the Book

The aim of the book is to allow anyone with no programming background to make exciting games for Windows.

Some of the areas that are covered in this book are the following:

- Learning game genres

- Designing games (and what good design is)

- Creating game sounds and music

- Creating and importing graphics for your games

- Using the Games Factory 2

- Creating the game *Future Tennis*

- Creating the game *Quick Draw*

- Creating the game *Last Pursuit*

- Learning about objects

- Learning about movement and animations

- Getting help

By the end of the book, you should be very comfortable with the Games Factory software and be able to begin to make your own game ideas a reality.

This book does *not* do the following:

- Teach you more complex programming languages like C++, C#, or Java, and it isn't meant to do so. This book is aimed at those people who want to make games easily without needing to learn those more complex languages. If you are interested in C++, then consider *C++ Programming Fundamentals* by Chuck Easttom.

- Teach you how to be a graphic artist or music creator. Look at *Composing Music for Video Games* by Andrew Clark or *3D Graphics Tutorial Collection* by Shamms Mortier.

- Show you how to become an Indie developer or build a team. If you want more information about being an Indie developer, read *The Indie Game Development Survival Guide* by David Michael.

- Assume that you are an expert at game creation. This book is aimed at those people with little or no knowledge of game creation, as well as those who might have an idea how things are put together but need more information.

- Show you how to make Windows-based applications—it is totally geared to games and game creation. If you want more information on making your own Windows applications, read *Power Users Guide to Windows Development* by Jason Darby.

Chapter Overview

This book flows in a simple, yet effective, order to allow you to get the most out of reading it. While it is possible to skip certain chapters, I highly recommended that you read through each chapter in the order that it is shown in the book. Here is a synopsis of what the book contains:

Chapter 1: Games—The book begins with a look at the different types of games that you might have played, called *game genres*.

Chapter 2: Game Design—This chapter details how you might come up with your game ideas and develop them into better ideas and a better structure before you begin making them.

Chapter 3: Graphics: Game Creation Essentials—This chapter provides information on different graphic settings, techniques, and features found in most Paint packages.

Chapter 4: Sound and Music—Here, you'll find reasons for using sound and music within your own creations and how to create and record them.

Chapter 5: Introduction to the Games Factory 2—This is an introduction to the game-making tool used in the book, the Games Factory 2. You will learn about its requirements, how to install it, and have a quick introduction to the basic terminology of the program.

Chapter 6: Behind the Scenes of the Games Factory 2—Before you begin to make your first game in TGF2, you will get a walk-through of the main editors and screens used in the program by looking at the game you will make in Chapter 7 called *Future Tennis*.

Chapter 7: Game Creation: Future Tennis—You'll make your first game here, which is a simple bat and ball game, and in so doing, you will learn a lot of the basic functionality of the Games Factory 2.

Chapter 8: Game Creation: Quick Draw—You will now make your second game, a game set in the Wild West called *Quick Draw*.

Chapter 9: Game Creation: Last Pursuit—Here is the third game created in the book, which shows how to make a car racing game.

Chapter 10: Advanced Control of Objects—You'll find that objects allow you to add extra features to your games, including high-score tables and text. You will learn about some of the objects you can use in your games.

Chapter 11: Working with Pictures and Animations in TGF2—You'll learn all about the built-in Picture Editor that allows you to import and draw your own images, as well as learning about the Animation Editor that animates your characters.

Chapter 12: Getting Help—You'll learn about which support, documentation, and program features are available to make your learning easier.

Chapter 13: Bug Finding and Fixing—This chapter focuses on bugs and how to test any games that you create for those elusive bugs. You will also learn how to use the built-in tool (the Debugger) within TGF2 to track down any programming problems.

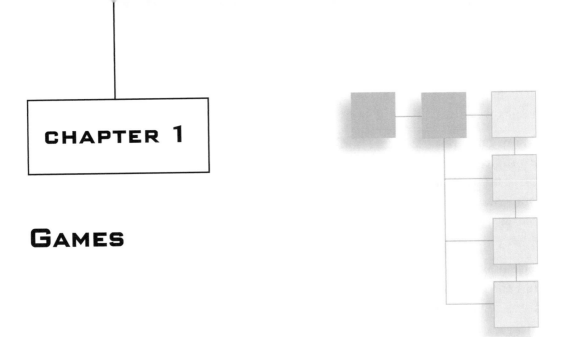

CHAPTER 1

GAMES

In this chapter:

- Why Make Games?
- 2D or 3D Games
- Game Types
- Chapter Summary

There's nothing more satisfying than loading up your favorite game and being transported to a world that no longer exists—maybe to the future, flying a spaceship, or even taking part in a sport that you could never conceive of doing in real life.

The games of today bear no resemblance to the first simple games that were made in the late '70s and '80s. Today, they have high-quality graphics and sound, complex stories, and, in some cases, million-dollar budgets, making the game industry more like the movie industry.

Unfortunately, making games is considered a black art in which you have to spend years learning how to program in complex machine languages before you can even get a simple graphic moving across the screen. Doesn't sound like much fun if you're just starting out, does it? Most of us want some immediate response from the computer, rather than spending a week just to get "Hello World" written on the screen. (The words "Hello World" are usually the first thing most programming books try to teach, and it's not very exciting.)

Many game programming books are aimed at the professional user market, for example, *Writing Games Using DirectX, Games Programming with C++,* and so on. The normal game-loving person doesn't fit into the professional category, but would love to fulfill his or her dreams of making a game. In fact, many people have aspirations to make games, but just don't know if it's possible to do so or where to start.

This book will show you how it is a lot easier than you may have thought to make fun and exciting games. It will also allow you to progress quickly and take an idea from concept to a fully playable game by the end of the book.

So let's begin our journey to learn how to make and design games the easy way!

Why Make Games?

There may be a number of reasons why you want to make games, and using the Games Factory 2 is a great way to achieve many of them. Some of the reasons why you want to make games might be the following:

- You are thinking of a career in games when you finish school.

- You want to make games for fun.

- Perhaps you are bored with playing games, and you want to make your own because you feel you might be able to do a better job.

- You want to re-create one of your favorite games.

- You want to make games for your friends and family.

2D or 3D Games

You may have heard of the terms *2D* (two-dimensional) or *3D* (three-dimensional) *games.* The terms refer to what dimension the game is being displayed in on-screen. Two-dimensional (2D) represents two coordinates on-screen: top to bottom and left to right, known as x and y. A 3D game uses three coordinates,

Table 1.1 A PC Games Chart

Game Name

Football Manager 2008
Call of Duty 4
Crysis
Half-Life 2 Orange Box
Unreal Tournament 3
The Sims 2
Gears of War
Need for Speed – ProStreet
Fifa Manager 08

meaning that objects can also be given a distance; these are known as x-, y-, and z-coordinates. Many casual games use 2D and many, if not most, "AAA" games are in 3D.

Casual Games versus AAA Games

Casual games are games that a user might only play for a small amount of time each session, that generally cost less to make, and that are cheaper to purchase than a normal AAA game. AAA games are the games you normally go into the computer games shop and see in the game chart. A game chart is a list of the top games for the month (see an example in Table 1.1).

This book is all about making 2D games and does not touch on 3D game creation aspects. The main reason for this is that you can get up and running much quicker making 2D games than 3D. We will talk about 2D and 3D games in Chapter 3, so if you don't fully understand the difference at the moment, then don't worry.

Game Types

Before we begin to look at how to develop and design your own games, we are going to take a quick look at the various game types that are played—some of which you might want to make, but also ones that your family and friends may like to play.

Platform

Most game players at some point have probably played a 2D-platform game like Sonic the Hedgehog or Mario (an example is shown in Figure 1.1). The player

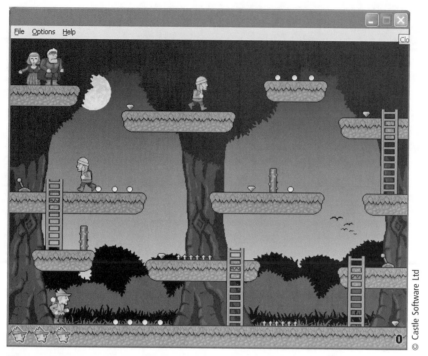

Figure 1.1
Robin is trying to rescue Maid Marian in this platform game.

usually has to navigate a series of platforms and ladders to reach a goal, which in the case of Figure 1.1 is to rescue Maid Marian.

Racing Car

Racing games center around the concept of driving around different tracks, collecting bonuses, and perhaps racing against a computer player. The great thing about racing car games is that you can add so much to the game, and it's pretty easy to think of new ideas for it. Car games could have weapons to destroy other cars, strange weather conditions, car upgrades to make them faster, single races, or tournaments. The full version of the Games Factory 2 comes with a number of car and track graphics to get you started.

You can see an example racing car game from the top view, made with the Games Factory, in Figure 1.2, and a 3D racing game called Forza 2 Motor Sport by Microsoft Games in Figure 1.3.

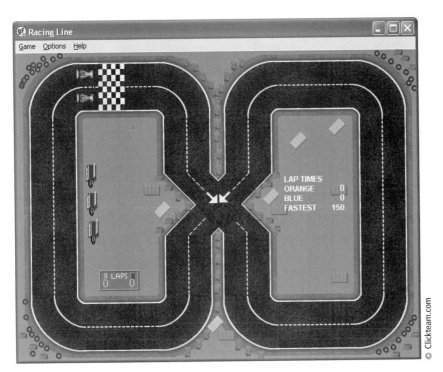

Figure 1.2
Classic racing car action in Racing Line.

Figure 1.3
3D car racing action in Forza 2 Motor Sport.

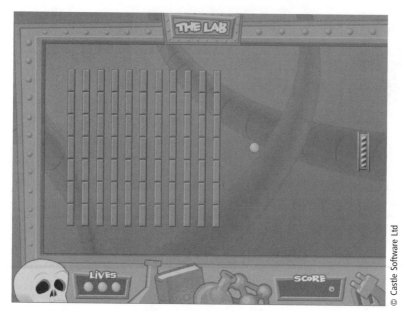

© Castle Software Ltd

Figure 1.4
Bat and ball action in the Lab.

Bat and Ball

A very popular type of game on early computers and still popular in the casual market is the bat and ball style of game, like Breakout or Pong (see example in Figure 1.4). You usually control a paddle and have to destroy blocks by using a bouncing ball. There have been many variations of this type of game over the years in which several things have changed: for example, the direction of the paddle/balls and various positive and negative effects when destroying certain blocks. There are even 3D versions.

Side-Scrolling Shoot-'Em-Ups

Shoot-'em-up games would normally have the gamer playing a space fighter pilot, who was defending the Earth against wave after wave of aliens (see Figure 1.5). The game could scroll from left to right or bottom to top, and it also could include bonuses for destroying a wave of enemy fighters, including shield and weapons upgrades. Very predictable stuff, but entertaining all the same.

Board Games

Chess, Solitaire, Monopoly, and Risk are just some examples of traditional board games that have been converted to the computer game format (see Figures 1.6

Figure 1.5
Side-scrolling shoot-'em-up in Saturn Storm.

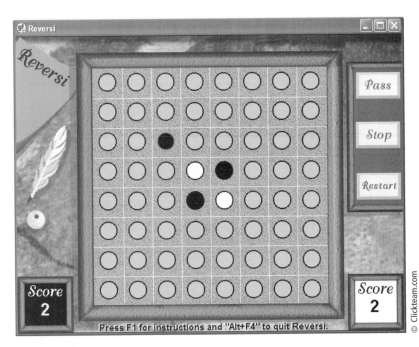

Figure 1.6
A classic board game of Reversi.

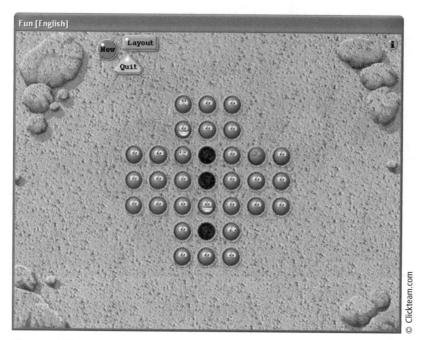

Figure 1.7
A new way of creating an old board game of Solitaire.

and 1.7). Board games that have been converted to the computer don't usually add much to the original concept except for video and graphic animations.

Card Games

Computer card games like Poker, Solitaire, and Hearts are very popular. The card game genre is very similar to board games, and it has experienced few innovations since it moved to the techie format. Many users don't play these games for fancy 3D graphics but for the challenge that this type of game can give them to play against. You can see a card game made using the Games Factory 2 in Figure 1.8.

Battle Card Games

Battle card games came about with the Magic: The Gathering craze, which spawned such card games as Pokémon and Yu-Gi-Oh. Battle card games play very much like traditional card games, only with pretty pictures and an emphasis on being collectible. Naturally, the decks are open-ended; if users buy more

Figure 1.8
A computer version of a simple card game.

cards, they become more powerful. Their move to the computer has been much like the traditional card games' move to the computer, with little real innovation.

Quiz Games

Quiz games are big, especially games such as Who Wants to Be a Millionaire and Deal or No Deal. The Games Factory 2 makes these games easy to create. The logic behind these so-called "multiple-choice games" is easy: All the games have to do is display a question and three or four answers. The hard part is researching and organizing all the content, questions, and answers. Quiz programs have become more interactive and can also contain video, sounds, and more interactivity between the player and the program. Figure 1.9 shows an example quiz game interface.

Puzzle Games

Puzzle games include Tetris, Mario, and others. Tetris, for example, involves game pieces falling from above, which players have to line up before they hit bottom. The player must fit them all together, in the most efficient manner, to

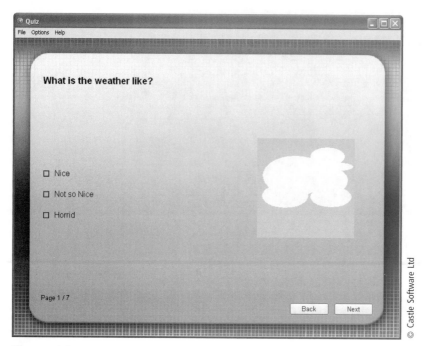

Figure 1.9
Typical quiz game interface.

leave no open spaces between the pieces. The pieces become more complex and fall faster as the game progresses.

Fighting Games

There are many fighting games: Street Fighter, Street Fighter 2, Renegade, and Golden Axe are just a few games that have a main fighting theme. The aim of the game is either to navigate a map or fight in an arena against other players or the computer. An example of a side-scrolling fighting game can be seen in Figure 1.10. Fighting games started as flat 2D worlds and now feature full 3D arenas and animated characters. The focus in a fighting game is the almost endless fighting moves and special moves you can use against your opponent.

Flight Sims

A flight simulator (sim) attempts to simulate real flying conditions by giving you control over such things as fuel, wind speed, and other instruments, as well as control over the flaps and wings of your craft. A sim will respond with the same limits as a real plane, as opposed to a simpler flying game, where you can't control much. A screenshot from a flight sim is shown in Figure 1.11.

Figure 1.10
The Kung Fu game is a fighting game made with the original Games Factory software.

Figure 1.11
Microsoft Flight Simulator X.

Turn-Based Strategy Games

In games such as X-Com, Heroes of Might and Magic, Civilization, and Masters of Orion, players take turns making moves. These games require a great deal of strategic thought and planning, much like Chess.

Real-Time Strategy Games

Command and Conquer 3, Age of Empires, Supreme Commander, and Caesar 4 are a few popular real-time strategy games. In these games, you don't have forever to take your turn before the next person moves. Faster players can make many moves in a short period of time. These games are also a bit like sims, since you are usually overseeing a large battle or war, as well as the building of towns and outposts. Resource management is important, such as in Command and Conquer, where you have to harvest (mine) ore called tiberium to be able to build more structures and soldiers. Two popular games, CivCity Rome and Stronghold, are shown in Figures 1.12 and 1.13, respectively.

© Firefly Studios

Figure 1.12
City building in the Roman Empire—CivCity Rome.

Figure 1.13
Castle-building strategy game—Stronghold.

Sims and Tycoons

These games include Sim City, Theme Hospital, Thrillville, and Zoo Tycoon. The most popular of the simulation games are games in which you run a town, world, ant colony, or a group of people, making decisions and managing resources. You can find tycoon games for any situation from running an ice cream parlour to running a zoo. These are often called "God games" because you are playing the part of God in the game world where you control all aspects of the game.

First-Person Shooter (FPS) 3D Games

These games include Dark Messiah, Half-Life 2, Halo, Doom 3, Quake, Far Cry, and Elder Scrolls IV Oblivion. The focus in these games is on technology and atmosphere. These games attempt to put you into the action, as you are literally looking out of the eyes of the character, seeing and hearing what the character sees or hears. As shown in Figure 1.14, the point of view is from a person looking at the action.

Third-Person 3D Games

Tomb Raider, Dark Vengeance, Zelda, and Fable are all third-person games. Although these are games in which you can switch from first- to third-person

Figure 1.14
Screenshot from Halo 2, a first-person 3D game.

Figure 1.15
Screenshot from Fable in third-person mode.

perspective, most are designed primarily to be one or the other. Tomb Raider in first person is not as much fun, since it is designed around seeing Lara Croft jump, roll, and tumble. In first person, you would not see these acrobatics. Figure 1.15 shows a third-person game. Notice how you can see the spell effects you cast (the protection circle) when in third-person mode. Likewise, when playing a first-person shooter, like Quake 3 Arena, you depend on speed and accuracy in battle to win, which is the point of the game. If you were able to play Quake 3 in third-person mode, you would die an awful lot since you would not be able to run, aim, shoot, and run some more as quickly.

RPGs (Role-Playing Games)

Ultima, Neverwinter Nights, and Dungeon Siege are all RPGs. These games emulate the traditional pen-and-paper games in which you play characters that have many significant attributes, such as health, intelligence, strength, and areas of knowledge and skill. RPGs generally allow you to create your own character and select the level of their attributes to create unique characters with specific skill sets.

Adventure Games

Broken Sword, CSI: Dark Motives, Sherlock Holmes and the Case of the Missing Earring, and Runaway 2: The Dream of the Turtle are all adventure games. In an adventure game, you walk around and try to fulfill a quest or unravel a mystery. You typically collect information and items. Battle is generally light and not the focus of this game type. The game is usually played using the mouse to point and click.

Full-Motion Video Games (FMVs)

FMV, or full-motion video, games include Myst, Riven, and . . . well, no other FMV game is worth mentioning. These games require a lot of art and animation or video production, and little of anything else. In an FMV, you mostly watch a movie and then select what portion of the movie to watch next, much like a computerized version of the "choose your own adventure" books. You select where you want to go, and the computer then knows which video to play next.

Educational and Edutainment Games

Some games or interactive products fall into this genre. Whether a game fits into this category depends mostly on its purpose, rather than on its content or use of technology. A first-person game would be an edutainment title if its intention were to educate and entertain, as would a quiz game. These genres are instructional and informative. The edutainment variety attempts to make learning fun,

Figure 1.16
Maths Magic educational game.

while the educational variety is straightforward learning. An example of an educational game can be seen in Figure 1.16.

Sports Games

Sports are a huge-selling genre, and those companies that own the licenses to such games release new versions on a yearly basis. In some cases, this is for a purely financial purpose (they get to sell a new version of a game every year rather than every three or four years for a typical game follow-up), but also this allows them to make their games accurate to ensure that the teams are up to date and contain the right players. You will find most popular sports are covered in the sports genre, including football (soccer), American football, basketball, ice hockey, and horse riding.

Screensavers/Desktop Toys

While not games, and not even very interactive for that matter, these products are generally entertaining, so they are usually lumped in with games and interactive products. These are fairly popular products you can make with the Games

© Castle Software Ltd

Figure 1.17
Micro Animals Fish screensaver.

Factory 2, like the screensaver in Figure 1.17, which was made for downloading a trial version and purchasing the full version for a small fee.

Chapter Summary

Now that we've touched upon game types, hopefully the creative juices are starting to flow, and you have some idea of what you would like to make and why you want to make it. Don't rush off just yet to begin making your game, because in the next chapter we will be looking at how to grow those simple ideas into full-blown games.

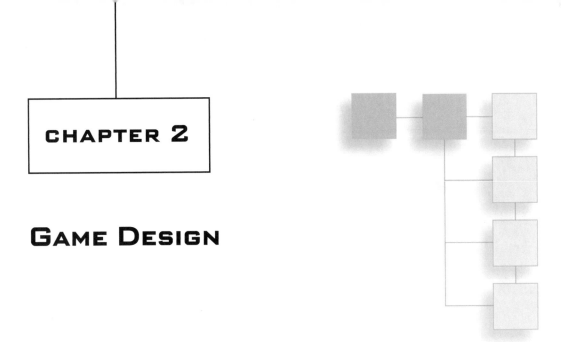

CHAPTER 2

GAME DESIGN

In this chapter:

- The Ideas
- The Story
- Game Mechanics
- Screen Design
- Chapter Summary

Before you get into learning about the Games Factory software and making your first sample games, you might want to consider what game you are making, how it is going to work, and its overall structure.

The Ideas

So you've got an idea! In fact, you probably have more than one idea. So which one should you choose to put all that time and effort into? You may have a lot of ideas flying around in your head, but you have to get a little bit more objective and realize that you can't implement them all at once.

The best way to do this is complete a simple table of game ideas, as shown in Table 2.1.

Table 2.1 Organizing Your Game Ideas

Game Type	Idea	Technology Concept	Rating	Difficulty
Car Racing	You are a budding racing driver looking at becoming a race champion. Before you can compete in the world championship, you need to win the regional heats.	Top-down scrolling	High	Medium
Flight Sim	You are a WWI pilot who has just joined your squadron and must take to the skies as soon as you arrive.	Story-driven 3D flight sim	Medium	High Impossible?
Scrolling	Aliens have invaded a small town in your local area. A band of citizens cannot stand by watching impending disaster. A small team armed with weapons goes in search of the alien menace.	Side scrolling	Low	Medium

Using this table, you will set out all of your current game ideas. Even if it's just a silly idea or a half thought-out concept, you should still write it down. Ideas shouldn't be judged at this point, so it's a good idea to keep notes of all game ideas so they are all in one place. The reason we make this table is to begin to reduce our ideas to a select few; that way, we can make in-roads into what we really want to make.

Split the table into five columns, which can easily be understood by just looking at them. This grouping is important because you never know when you might need to go back to the table for ideas. Although the table is simplistic, that's OK. At this stage, you don't want to get into any great detail since that would mean writing a lot more information down, which is something you don't want to do right now. Later on, you will expand the ideas behind the games that deserve more time and effort.

The columns are separated as follows:

- **Type:** This categorizes the game type into one of the standard gaming groups. For example: RPG, war game, flight simulation, isometric, FPS, and so on.

- **Idea:** This is just a brief overview of what the game is about. Because you won't need to go into much detail at this stage, you are keeping it simple. It's just a quick overview of the story and what the aim of the game is.

- **Technology**: What game technology will the game use? This could be top-down scrolling, side scrolling, 3D first person, and so on. This gives you an idea of what might be required from the tool you intend to use to make your game. For example, it's not a good idea to make a 3D first person shooter game if the product you're choosing can only make 2D games.

- **Rating**: How high do you rate your idea? How excited are you at the prospect of making this game? If it's a low rating, then it's not worth spending time and effort to make it because you will probably get bored and give up. Instead, we want you to get to the end of your game happy in the knowledge that you saw it through to the end!

- **Difficulty**: It's time to be honest about your skills in your chosen game-making product. Many people come into the game-making forums who have never used a game-making product before and want to make an online role-playing game or something similar, which is just too complex for a first game idea. If you really think your game idea is too difficult, then put it aside, because you don't want to start on a project and then struggle with the concepts. This advice is meant to make your life easier and not for you to deceive yourself into thinking you can make anything you want to. There is no shame in admitting an idea is too difficult at this stage, because at a later time it might not be, and you still have the idea down on paper.

After you have looked through the table and found which is the highest-rated game that strikes you as the most interesting (there may be more than one idea that is rated high), then you are ready to continue.

Rating Your Game

Remember to use the Difficulty column to decide between multiple high-ranking game ideas.

The Story

It is very difficult to be unique with regard to stories these days, since many things have already been tried. Your story doesn't have to be unique or new as long as the idea works well. Make sure that you spend some time writing your story, which is the key to what will be included in your game. Also, spell check your story and any material that other people will see. If you are making a game that you will upload to your Web site, it is best to make sure everything is spell checked before you upload it and make a Web page to detail what the game is about. If an Internet user sees anything that looks amateurish (with many spelling mistakes), then he will probably decide not to download the demo/game. The Internet is full of buggy software, viruses, and spyware so users are scared to download anything that might contain dubious content. They are more likely to think that your software might contain one of the above if there are many spelling mistakes. It really is amazing how you can influence the quality of your product simply by checking some of the smallest details.

You now need to flesh out your story to get a fuller picture of what it's all about. It might help to make some notes of what is going to be contained in the game. This is called the *story plan*. The story plan is a simple document that details some of the main key elements of the story and what it will contain. (You don't need to go into too much detail now because you are just trying to bring out the flavor of the story/content.)

This story plan is just an exercise to make sure you have an idea that you ultimately like. Once you have done the story plan, you might find that you no longer like the idea and you don't want to make it. If that's the case, then you have "succeeded," because you shouldn't be making games you don't like.

From the list of game ideas created previously, let's pick "car racing" as an example of how to create a story plan. So the story plan should go something like Table 2.2.

Even at this stage, you have an idea of what your game is all about and what things are contained in it, including the following:

- Six regional heats—in various locations

- One final track—after you have progressed through the heats

- Car upgrades

- Track obstacles

- Prizes

- Car repairs

- Computer-controlled drivers

- A dangerous sport

Table 2.2 Story Plan

Game Name	Car Racing
Story	After working seven years at the local carting center (where you practiced your driving skills in your lunch hour), you are now convinced you can compete in the world's deadliest and most dangerous racing event, "Death Racer." Unfortunately, entry to the event is very competitive, and people have to compete in the regional heats for a chance to be in the ultimate racing event and win the coveted prize
Initial Game Details	You will need to complete six regional heats (tracks) and be in the top 10 drivers to be promoted to the Death Racer event.
	You will get points if you appear in the top three of each of these regional heats. Additionally, you will be awarded cash prizes, which you can spend on car upgrades or a new vehicle.
	If you come in last in any regional heat, the game will end.
	The Death Racer event is one track, which contains some of the most dangerous obstacles that you come across in the whole game.
	In total, there are 50 drivers competing in the heats. The top 10 drivers with the most points get promoted to the Death Racer. There are computer-controlled heats in which you will not compete but the computer will generate the results.

Now you have your initial story idea and the basic game details. Break the game down further so it is easy to understand what needs to be included within the game you are about to make. Using the list of items generated from your story plan, you need to get into some more detail by creating a game list. This list will then be your starting point for creating the game. After the game is created, you will need to review it and decide whether or not to remove or add extra items.

So it's time to brainstorm. Write down every game idea you can think of and don't be afraid of putting down too much at this point, even if the idea is far from good or ideal. The list is very useful for confirming all of the things you want in the game.

So let's take a look at your game list:

```
Dangerous Racing
Weapons
        Forward Firing Missile
        Rear Firing Missile
        Laser
        Mine
Obstacles
```

```
            Oil Slick
            Water
Fall Off Track
Weather
            Snow
            Rain
            Sunny

Car Improvements

Engine
            Speed (Turbo)
            Power
            Bodywork
            Durability
            Damage
            Other Cars Bounce Off
            Tires
            Breaking
            Cornering
            Affected by Oil, Water, and Track Conditions
```

This is just a small example of a game list, but it could, in theory, run into many pages. You don't need to write many pages—this is just a good way of getting ideas for your game, so don't worry if you run out of ideas after only half a page. If some of the items are too difficult to code or maybe just too much work to do, you can always mark them for something you can add in a future version.

Game Mechanics

The final stage of generating the story and game mechanics is to take your final list of items into the game and begin to make them computer specific. What this means is to actually begin to write down the boundaries of each object that will be in the game. Some examples of this might be the following: What are the normal maximum speeds of the cars, how much do items from the garage cost, and how many levels can the cars be upgraded?

This part of the documentation is quite detailed and in-depth, so you do need to have some patience when creating the list. It will speed up your game programming greatly and will reduce the amount of time needed to think about how the game works.

Let's look at a couple of examples of detailing the mechanics of the game.

Car Types

At various stages of the game, you will be able to purchase a new car or upgrade your current one.

Cars will have various starting stats, which can then be upgraded, but each car will have limits on how far it can be improved.

An example of the breakdown from the description can be seen in Table 2.3.

You can then break this list down even further to detail each specific level of component so that it's also easy to program when you get to that point. An example of a further breakdown is shown in Table 2.4.

Table 2.3 Car Levels

Car Type	Engine Start	Tire Start	Speed Start	Bodywork Start	Cost
X1	Lvl −1	Lvl −1	Lvl −1	Lvl −1	Default
Speeder	Lvl −1	Lvl −2	Lvl −1	Lvl −1	$15,000
Hoffe-E1	Lvl −2	Lvl −2	Lvl −1	Lvl −1	$20,000
Panther	Lvl −1	Lvl −2	Lvl −2	Lvl −2	$35,000
Turbo-x	Lvl −2	Lvl −2	Lvl −3	Lvl −2	$55,000
Win Fusion	Lvl −2	Lvl −3	Lvl −3	Lvl −2	$70,000
Etc...					

Table 2.4 Car Engine Speeds

Engine Speed Level	Top Speed
Lvl −1	8 mph
Lvl −2	12 mph
Lvl −3	15 mph
Lvl −4	17 mph
Lvl −5	19 mph
Lvl −6	22 mph
Lvl −7	24 mph
Lvl −8	27 mph
Lvl −9	30 mph
Lvl −10	35 mph

You're probably thinking what a lot of work this is going to be, but in all honesty, for a simple game, it might only take five minutes. For a bigger game, it might take a few hours or even days to document the features of what's going to be in the game. Without detailed game mechanics and story information, while programming the game you're going to spend a lot more time trying to get it to function correctly.

Screen Design

As you have now completed the story and game mechanics, you will need to understand how the game is going to look. This will give you an idea of what each screen or level will look like. Doing this step allows you to cast a designer's eye over the recommended structure and ensures that everything works correctly from a usability and layout point of view. If you are getting a friend to make your graphics, then the screen design is for their benefit also. You should create the designs how you want them to look and then send them off to a graphics person to be generated.

Changing Focus

You may find that you change parts of your game mechanics while doing your screen design. This is OK, and both are interchangeable as far as the order in which you do them.

Game Map

The game map is a simple yet effective way of breaking your game up into sections, levels, or areas of the game. This will also include main menus, level menus, end-of-game screens, or high-score tables. Using a single letter-sized piece of paper (you may need to stick more together), you will map out the main parts to your game and where they link (shown in Figure 2.1).

You can see from the diagram how each screen connects and how it relates to other screens around it. On each box within the game map, there should be a number. This number signifies which picture is on the screen map (see the next section).

Screen Map

The screen map takes the process to the next level, where you start to draw each screen. This is the detailed part of the drawing process, and it could take a while

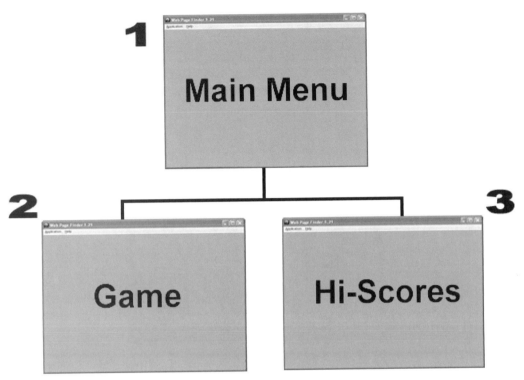

Figure 2.1
Game map showing connections between screens.

for you to complete it. It is very important, though, as this makes you think about what each screen will look like and which components of the game will appear and where. (See Figure 2.2 for an example of a screen map using computer graphics rather than just pencil drawings.)

You may actually find that when you do this, you will suddenly realize that there isn't any room left to put other graphics in, or it just doesn't work on paper! This is another step that makes it easier to design your game before writing any part of the game.

Placeholder Graphics

You can draw the screen map on the computer using placeholder graphics. These are graphics that may have the same shape and size as the final graphics you might want to use in your game. That way you can set up a fake screen that gives you an idea of the layout.

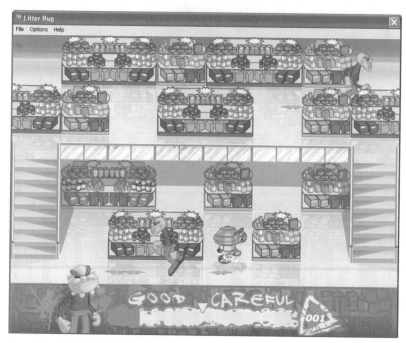

Figure 2.2
A screen map details everything on each screen.

Chapter Summary

Now that you have made a list of all the items in your game, the mechanics, and how it will look on-screen, you are nearly ready to learn how to use the Games Factory 2 to make your creations come to life. First, let's look at the main components that you will add into your games, which include graphics, sounds, and music.

CHAPTER 3

GRAPHICS: GAME CREATION ESSENTIALS

In this chapter:

- Visual Elements

- Basic Elements of an Image

- Manipulating Images

- Advanced Image Manipulation

- Chapter Summary

To create games, you will need to learn about the elements that make up a game, sights, and sounds. This chapter discusses the core building blocks that exist in every modern game. For this chapter, we will be learning all about the visual aspect of games: the graphics, sprites, pictures, and images.

Visual Elements

When talking about visual elements, we are obviously talking about what you see on the screen during gameplay. In any major production, from a Web site to a game, the layout of the screens and the graphic images to make them are very important. In a large development team, a number of people—including a designer, producer, art director, and others—usually work on them. In a one- or two-person development effort, you might be performing all of these roles.

Creating the assets you will use to make interface elements may require the use of many software tools and techniques. These assets are often sketched on paper first or mocked up on the computer. Some of the tools you can use are 2D paint programs that work only with flat images, 3D programs that allow you to build and render objects that realistically re-create a 3D environment or object, and even digital photographs and scans. To create the images, you will need to have an understanding of the concepts of the images and a grasp of the tools you will be using.

The 2D art assets you might create include, but are not limited to, the following:

- **Menu screens**: Look at the toolbar in your word processor, browser, or favorite game, and you will see art that was created by an artist.

- **Credit screens**: These screens often contain art such as logos, images, and even fonts or special letters unique to the product, people, and company they represent.

- **Logos for companies, products, and services**: Logos can be simple letters, 2D masterpieces, or fully rendered 3D scenes. Look on the Web, and you will see logos that range from clip art to actual pieces of art.

- **User interfaces:** These are broken down into background images, buttons, cursors, and other art objects a user must click or interact with. You may also hear them called *graphical user interfaces* (sometimes called *GUIs*).

- **In-game assets:** These include the textures on the walls, the floors, and the characters. Even the 3D models and objects have 2D art applied to them.

Early computers did not display graphics; they were limited to alphanumeric characters, such as letters, punctuation marks, and numbers. Surprisingly, games were still made on these primitive machines. When computers started including graphics cards, games started their move toward the amazing graphics you see today. Games have pushed the development of the computer as gamers demanded (and were willing to pay for) faster chips, better graphics cards, and better sound.

Let's look at the core technology a computer artist deals with every day. In computer graphics today, there are two basic types of art: 2D and 3D. All 2D, or two-dimensional, art consists of a flat image with no depth; 3D, or three-dimensional, art shows depth, as illustrated in Figure 3.1.

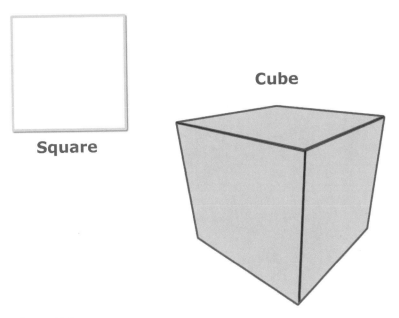

Figure 3.1
A square is 2D, while a cube is 3D.

The three dimensions in 3D art are described in the Cartesian coordinate system, using x-, y-, and z-coordinates. This may be one of the most surprising aspects of game development; you can actually use some of the math topics you learned in school! In fact, algebra, geometry, and physics all play a role in game making. Simply stated, in the Cartesian coordinate system, x represents the distance along a horizontal line (or axis), y represents the distance along a vertical line, and z represents the distance backward and forward (see Figures 3.2, 3.3, and 3.4).

Basic Elements of an Image

To properly understand 2D images, you must understand a few things about the basic elements that comprise those images, as discussed next.

Pixel

We'll start with the most basic element of an image—the *pixel*, or picture element. A pixel is a colored dot on the screen. A computer image is made up of pixels arranged in rows and columns. See Figure 3.5 for an illustration of a pixel. No matter how big and fancy a computer image is or what has been done to it, it's all just a bunch of pixels.

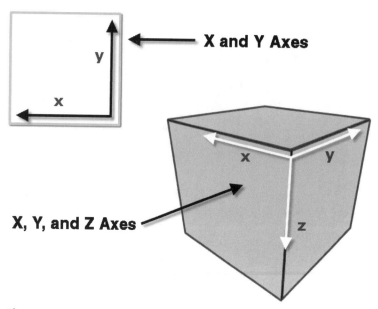

Figure 3.2
The Cartesian coordinate system. The x, y, and z axes.

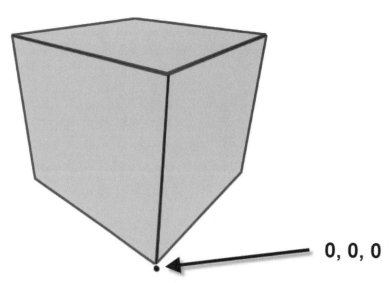

Figure 3.3
A cube and the xyz value of its location in space.

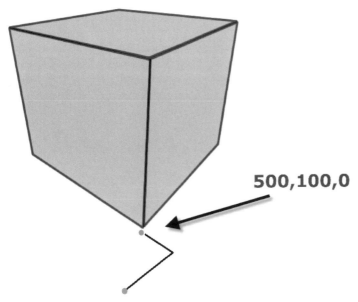

500,100,0

Figure 3.4
Another cube in a different xyz position.

After an image has been created with a particular number of pixels, the maximum detail is set and cannot be increased. The image can be enlarged, and the number of pixels can be increased by a mathematical process called *interpolation,* as illustrated in Figures 3.6 and 3.7. However, this does not increase the detail; it simply adds extra pixels to smooth the transition between the original pixels.

Resolution

Resolution is the number of pixels displayed (width × height) in an image. A typical computer monitor displays 75 to 90 dpi (dots per inch, which refers to the number of pixels per inch in an image). A printed image usually needs to be 300 dpi or more to look good in print. Often, when computer people receive an image from a person who is used to working in print, they are surprised when the one-inch icon they requested takes up a *huge* number of bytes, but the image is still one inch by one inch. The reason for the enormous size is that a print person is used to using and saving images at a higher dpi. Some of the most common screen resolutions are: 640 × 480, 800 × 600, 1024 × 768, 1152 × 864, and 1280 × 1024. An 800 × 600 resolution means that the screen is 800 pixels wide (horizontal) and 600 pixels high (vertical). See the examples in Figures 3.8, 3.9, and 3.10.

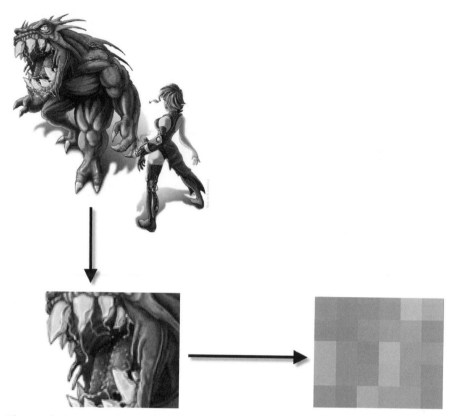

Figure 3.5
A pixel is the smallest unit of a computer image—simply colored dots.

Figure 3.6
An area of the image before enlarging.

Figure 3.7
The same area enlarged with pixels interpolated.

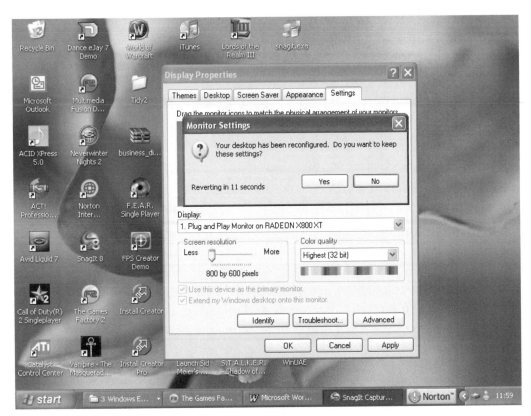

Figure 3.8
The Windows desktop at 800 × 600 dots per inch.

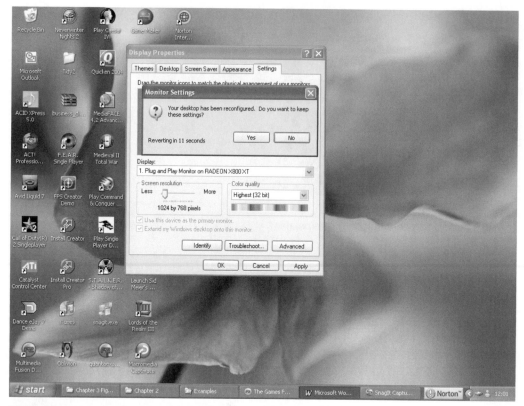

Figure 3.9
The Windows desktop at 1024 × 768 dots per inch.

Colors

When working with most interactive content, you need to understand how color works in the computer. In some situations, such as games and Web sites, you will need precise control over your colors to achieve the effects you want. Colors are usually specified as RGB values, and artists may sometimes give you the specific value to use for a color in an image. An RGB value (also known as the *indexed color value*) is the mixture of red, green, and blue to make other colors, just as in art class when you mixed red and yellow paint to make orange.

The first number represents red, the second represents green, and the third represents blue. These values range from 0 to 255. For example, 255,0,0 means you have all red and no green or blue, black would be 0,0,0 (no colors at all), and white would be 255,255,255 (all colors at their highest intensity). In Figures 3.11 through 3.13, you can see the RGB values of the colors, and even though the images are in black and white, you can see the position of the marker in the color palette.

Figure 3.10
The Windows desktop at 1280 × 1024 dots per inch.

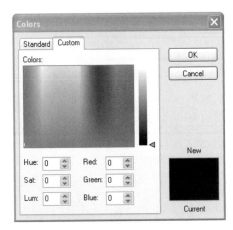

Figure 3.11
The RGB color palette for black.

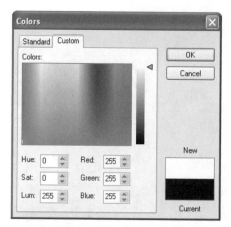

Figure 3.12
The RGB color palette for white.

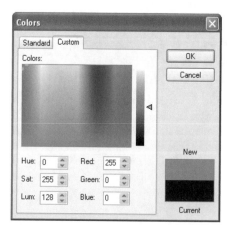

Figure 3.13
The RGB color palette for red.

You will also hear *color* referred to as CMYK. CMYK is a mode used by traditional printing processes and stands for cyan, magenta, yellow, and black. You'll almost certainly never use CMYK color in game and computer content creation—you'll always deal in RGB or indexed color.

Number of Colors

A computer video card can display a certain number of colors at a time—16 or 256 at the low end, or even thousands or millions at the high end (see Figures 3.14 to 3.17). *Color depth* describes how many colors your screen can

Figure 3.14
An image in eight colors. See the images located in the figures folders on the companion CD to see a color version of this image.

Figure 3.15
An image in 16 colors. See the images located in the figures folders on the companion CD to see a color version of this image.

Figure 3.16
An image in 256 colors. See the images located in the figures folders on the companion CD to see a color version of this image.

Figure 3.17
An image in millions of colors. See the images located in the figures folders on the companion CD to see a color version of this image.

display at once, in terms of *bits*, and refers to the amount of memory used to represent a single pixel. The most common values are 8-bit, 16-bit, 24-bit, and 32-bit color; the more bits, the wider the range of displayable colors.

The interesting thing about these four images is that the colors used in the images will determine the number of pixels required. Visibly there is no difference between Figures 3.19 and 3.20, but there is about a 3.5 MB difference in file size. True Color (24-bit color) can display about 16.8 million colors for each pixel on the screen. The human eye cannot distinguish the difference between that many colors. High Color (16-bit color) displays between 32,000 and 64,000 colors. However, this is still a very impressive range of colors, and enough for most work. The 256 Color setting is more limited. It stores its color information in a palette. Each palette can be set to contain any of thousands or millions of different color values, but the screen can't show more than 256 different colors at once.

Very few (if any) games still use this more limited color palette because, as with increased resolution, having more colors means the images look better and have a much better quality.

Manipulating Images

During the development of your project, you will have to manipulate images to get them to fit your needs. The basics of image manipulation are similar to the text editing you may have done in your word processor. Commands such as Cut, Copy, and Paste are common. We will also look at Skew, Rotate, Resize, Crop, and Flip.

- **Cut.** If you cut an image, you remove it from the scene, as shown in Figure 3.18. But don't worry, you can paste it back or undo your action.

- **Copy.** Copy does not alter your image; it creates a copy in the memory of your computer that you can paste somewhere else.

- **Paste.** As mentioned previously, after cutting or copying an image, you can paste it somewhere else.

- **Skew.** Some image manipulation programs allow you to skew (slant, deform, or distort) an image, as shown in Figure 3.19.

- **Rotate.** Rotating is self-explanatory; you can free-rotate an image or rotate it precisely a certain amount, as shown in Figure 3.20.

Copy   Paste   Cut

Figure 3.18
Cutting and copying sections of an image. Copying does not affect the original image.

Figure 3.19
Skewing an image.

Figure 3.20
Rotating an image.

- **Resize.** Resizing an image is useful, but be careful. Any severe manipulation of an image degrades it, and resizing can do a lot of damage.

Watch Out for Degradation

If you reduce an image and then enlarge it again, you will seriously degrade it. This is because, in effect, you are enlarging a small image. The degradation takes place when you reduce an image and when you enlarge it (see Figures 3.21, 3.22, and 3.23).

- **Crop.** Cropping cuts an image to a smaller area you define, as shown in Figures 3.24 and 3.25.

- **Flip (horizontal and vertical).** You can flip images horizontally and vertically (see Figures 3.26, 3.27, and 3.28).

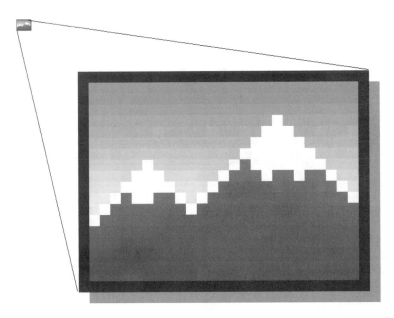

Figure 3.21
A smaller image blown up; pixel rip.

Figure 3.22
An image reduced.

Figure 3.23
The same image enlarged to its original size. Notice what this has done.

Figure 3.24
Cropping an image. The crop outline.

Figure 3.25
The image cropped. Everything outside the crop outline is now gone.

Figure 3.26
The image.

Figure 3.27
The image flipped horizontally.

Figure 3.28
The image flipped vertically.

Advanced Image Manipulation

In the last section, we looked at some basic image editing operations, and only scratched the surface of what you'll need to do to create graphics for a game. Here are some more advanced terms.

Sprites

A sprite is a graphic image that can move within a larger image. In your games, these might be characters, buttons, and other items. Notice that the sprite image in Figure 3.29 has a single-color border around it, and in Figure 3.30, the surrounding color part is not seen.

Figure 3.29
A sprite image. Notice the solid color part surrounding the image.

Figure 3.30
A sprite image in a game. Notice that the solid part is not displayed; you can see the background.

Sprite animation is done just like cartoon animation. A series of images is played in sequence to make it appear that a character is walking or a logo is spinning, for instance. Figure 3.31 shows examples of sprite frames.

Masking

A mask is a special image that is used to "mask" off portions of another image. A mask works like a stencil—it lets you paste a nonrectangular image into another image. When you paste a mask into another image, it overlays whatever was in the image at the spot where the mask is pasted (see Figures 3.32, 3.33, and 3.34).

image 0   image 1   image 2

image 3   image 4   image 5

Figure 3.31
A series of sprite images for a spinning graphic object.

Figure 3.32
An image of a card dealer.

Figure 3.33
The mask for the card dealer image.

Figure 3.34
The mask and image combined in a scene.

Color Masking

You can also use masking to specify that a specific color should be rendered as clear or transparent. Game programmers usually choose something like a bright pink or green that they most likely will not use anywhere else in the game art.

Transparency

You can also display images in games as halfway between solid and clear (as shown in Figures 3.35 and 3.36). To determine transparency, the computer looks at each pixel in the image and at the pixel directly under it. It then creates a new pixel that is a blended value of the original pixels (see Figures 3.35 and 3.36).

Anti-Aliasing

Look closely at the computer-generated images in Figures 3.37, 3.38, and 3.39. See those jagged edges on the letters? They look jagged, as if they are all a solid color. However, by using various shades of a color and gradually blending the edge color with the background color, the computer can make the transition smooth and fool the eye from a distance. The technique called *anti-aliasing* is one of the reasons why images with more colors look better. With more colors, you can blend them more gradually. This is also the reason why using a higher resolution (more pixels) makes an image look better—the blending is smoother between pixels.

Figure 3.35
The masked card dealer image with transparency set at 50%.

Figure 3.36
A close-up detail of the image.

Figure 3.37
This image has no anti-aliasing.

Graphic Formats

Graphic images are stored in many different formats, for many reasons. The main reason for selecting a particular graphic format is usually the image quality and the usefulness of the format for the particular job you are doing. Some image formats produce very large files because they retain a lot of image data, while

Figure 3.38
This image has anti-aliasing.

Figure 3.39
Here is a close-up of both of the images' edges.

some formats can compress an image and strip out data for a smaller file size. Still other formats degrade images (in an acceptable way) so they can be very small, for uses such as Web sites. Figures 3.40 and 3.41 show two versions of an image. The degradation is very good considering that the file size of the BMP image is almost 20 times the file size of the JPG image.

Figure 3.40
This 640 × 480 image is in BMP format and is 900K.

Figure 3.41
This 640 × 480 image is a compressed JPEG and is only 68K.

Chapter Summary

This chapter looked at the basic elements of images and how they were created. Now that you are familiar with graphics, you are almost ready to start creating content for a game. In the next chapter, you'll learn about music and sound effects.

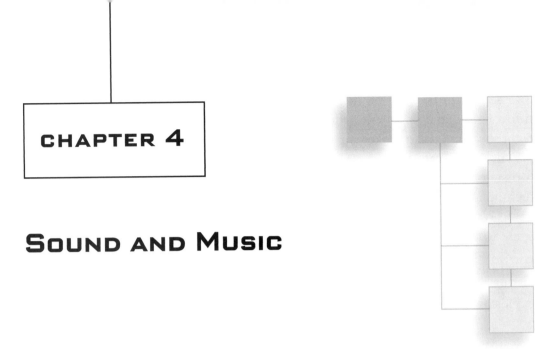

CHAPTER 4

Sound and Music

In this chapter:

- Why Sound and Music Are Important

- Obtaining or Creating Sounds and Music

- Recording Sounds

- Creating Music

- Chapter Summary

Of the many components that go into making a video game, perhaps none gets less attention than music and sound effects. Adding good quality music and sound effects is one of the best ways to add production value to your games. You'll find many different software and low-cost hardware available to help you make or create believable sound effects, and music will greatly enhance the game player's enjoyment of the game.

Why Sound and Music Are Important

If you think about watching a silent movie (a film with no sound), you may find that your overall enjoyment of the film is affected because of the lack of sound, not only from the words that people speak, but also from the lack of sound and music. If you consider movies like the *Matrix* and *Lord of the Rings,* which have great sound tracks, consider how much you would enjoy them without any sound.

The same can be said for the computer game market, and adding sound and music into games is as important as creating graphics and gameplay. With the right sound, you can make your game feel more real or atmospheric. Perhaps you are making a scary game for Halloween; the game would be scarier if there were footsteps, a howling dog, and screams. Professional games also employ this technique to give the player a sense of really being in the world. In the online game World of Warcraft, there are noises played when walking, when creating a spell, when fighting and creating items, and so on.

What you hear in a game can be recorded (or sampled) sounds, such as voices and music; menu sounds like beeps and button clicks; and other effects, such as explosions, weapons fire, footsteps, and a long list of other in-game sound effects.

Obtaining or Creating Sounds and Music

You don't have to come up with all the sounds yourself. Just as musicians buy CDs with loops, you can buy sound effects libraries. These libraries include sounds that will work directly, or with modification, with the vast majority of sound effects.

Creating unique sounds, or doing your own sounds, is often a very simple process. If you have a personal digital assistant (PDA) or a portable recorder of some sort, you can often record the sounds yourself. For instance, if you have a game with animals, a visit to a pet store or local zoo is often all you will need to add the appropriate noises. If you are creating a sports title, visiting a local sporting event will give you all the crowd and background noises you would ever need.

Stock Up on Sounds

> If you visit local areas to record sounds, keep in mind that you often need more than you think you do. For example, the sounds may not be the quality you need, or after editing, you may only have a few usable minutes from a 10-minute segment. Always try to get more material than you think you'll need.

The other basic type of sound effect for a game is the effect that occurs when some type of action happens. These sounds can take a great deal of time to produce and may require a tremendous amount of specialized equipment. Fortunately, as you'll see next, with a little effort and some common items, you can use some very simple ideas to record these types of sounds for your games.

Recording Sounds

It doesn't really matter what type of device you use to record sounds; ultimately, you have to get the data into the computer. For this setup, assume that you are using a tape recorder, a digital recorder, or a PDA. In this section, you'll see how to connect these devices to the sound or microphone inputs on the computer's sound card, and how to change the sounds into a digital form.

How to Record

The first step is to create the recordings. For the games you'll be creating in this book, we have already provided you with the music and sounds. What if you are making your own game and you want to make your own sounds? With this in mind, you might need to create effects for a variety of sounds, such as gunshots, footsteps, and perhaps collision noises. These are actually quite easy to record.

In Table 4.1, you will see a list of several types of actions you can easily record with common household items. You can use this list, or change it, so you can come up with sounds for many types of games.

Table 4.1 How to Record Sounds Using Household Items

Sound Type	How to Record
Car Crash	Fill a box with scrap metal and chunks of wood. Shake vigorously.
Fire	Take a piece of cellophane and crinkle it with your hands.
Door Slamming	Place the recording device near the door hinges and slam the door. You could also open and close the door slowly to get a different sound.
Body Collisions	Strike an item such as a pumpkin or watermelon with a piece of wood or a rubber mallet. Try various methods to get the right sound. As there is a potential for a mess to be created, it's probably best not to do this indoors.
Rain	Record the sound of rain on a roof or metal sheet. If it's not currently raining, you can simulate the effect. Cut the bottoms of five plastic cups into different shapes, such as a square, star, or ellipse. Tape the cuts together and then pour uncooked rice into the top of the cups. This will sound like rain falling.
Thunder	As with rain, you could wait for a storm to record it. If you don't get many storms where you live or you don't want to wait for one, you can simulate it. Get a piece of sheet metal and shake/wobble it to create the sound.
Footsteps	The best way to record this is by using the real thing. For outdoors, walk on a gravel area, and for indoors, walk on a hardwood floor to produce the best sounds.
Machines	If possible, record the actual machine noises. For instance, if you are creating a racing game, go to a race and record the sounds. Other sounds that work well are vacuum cleaners, saws, drills, or hammers. You may need help from an adult to obtain these sounds, depending on the device.
Gunshots	Hit a leather seat with a thin wooden stick. For different types of sounds, experiment by hitting other materials with the stick.

Permissions for Sounds

Recording sounds can be a lot of fun, but you might need to get permission to obtain some of them or be careful not to damage any items that you use.

For ideas about experimentation, consider gunshots. As mentioned previously, you can hit a leather seat with a thin wooden stick. Strike various objects and use sticks of varying strengths. Creating sound effects is very much trial and error, so spend time finding several objects that sound good and record all of them.

Using a PDA

The next step is to connect your recorder to the computer. If you are using a Pocket PC or Windows CE-based PDA, you can simply connect it to the computer and transfer the recordings, which will already be in WAV format.

Depending on the sound quality of your PDA, the sounds may or may not be of value. If they are not good quality, you will need to find a different recording device or attach a microphone to your computer.

Using a Recording Device

If you are using a tape recorder, mini-disc recorder, or other recording device, you will have to attach it to your computer's sound card. Most sound cards have four connectors: Line In, Line Out, Microphone, and MIDI/Game Port. Figure 4.1 shows the layout of a typical sound card.

Most modern sound cards may not have a MIDI port or game port, as many devices now use USB connections.

Figure 4.1
The layout of a typical sound card.

The following list explains the various connectors:

- **MIDI/Game Port:** The port most commonly used to connect a game paddle or joystick to the computer. This port also lets you connect a MIDI (*Musical Instrument Digital Interface*) device, such as a keyboard, to the computer.

- **Line In:** A connector that lets you connect a sound source to the computer. Examples include CD players, tape recorders, and other recording devices.

- **Line Out:** A connector that allows you to connect the computer to anything that accepts sound input. Used most commonly for speakers or headphones.

- **Microphone:** A connector that lets you connect a microphone to record your own sound files. If necessary, you can also connect a recording device to this port.

After you have located the Line In or Mic (microphone) connection, attach your device to the computer. Depending on the device, you may need different types of cables and connectors. The majority of sound cards use 1/8" (miniplug) jacks for Mic and Line In.

Using Your Sound Card's Mixer Panel

After connecting the device, you will need to open up the Windows Volume program. The type of sound card and software you have will determine if you can access this from the system tray (located in the bottom right of your toolbar) or from the Sound and Audio option in the Control Panel. The icon on the system tray will look something like Figure 4.2. You can double left-click it, single right-click and select Open Volume Control, or access the option through the Control Panel. You will get a standard sound card mixer panel, as shown in Figure 4.3.

Figure 4.2
The sound control icon shown in the system tray.

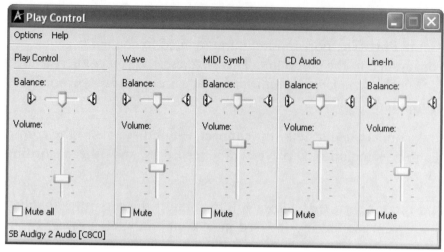

Figure 4.3
The mixer panel allows you to choose options related to the sound card.

Sound Differences for Vista and XP

The Sound and Audio option is available in the Control Panel for Windows XP users. For Vista, you will need to access the Control Panel and then the option Hardware and Sound, which looks very different from Windows XP.

When you first open the mixer, you will see all the possible playback volumes. Set the volumes as follows.

1. If the Wave Balance (the second slider from the left in Figure 4.3) is checked, click the Mute box to uncheck it.

2. Make sure the Wave Balance slider and the Play Control Balance slider (the leftmost one in Figure 4.3) are both at least halfway up.

Next, set the sound card's recording devices.

1. Choose Options | Properties.

2. In the box labeled Adjust Volume For, select Recording. Each of the devices from which your sound card can record will be listed in the window.

3. Click OK. This will display the Recording Control window.

4. Make sure that the volume of the category you plan to use is halfway up. For instance, if you are using the Microphone, ensure that Microphone is halfway up.

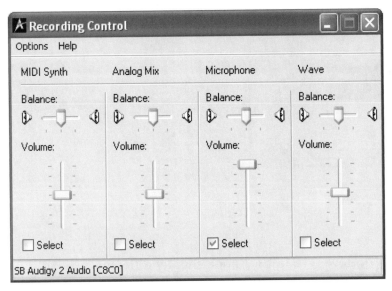

Figure 4.4
Microphone with the correct settings.

Figure 4.4 shows the Recording Control, as it should appear.

Using Windows Sound Recorder

A simple way to record sounds for your games is to use the built-in Windows sound recorder software and a microphone. The quality of the sound will depend on the quality of your microphone and whether you can filter out any other noise in your environment. This is a good way to create simple sounds to give you an idea of how your final game might be before you record better or more professional sounds. In creating computer games, developers usually put "markers" in the game. A marker can be a simple sound or a graphic that represents the voice recordings or graphics that have yet to be created.

So you can use Windows sound recorder as an easy and inexpensive (because the only additional equipment required is a microphone) way to get sound into your game, or as a temporary measure if you plan to create or buy better sounds later.

1. Click Start | All Programs | Accessories | Entertainment | Sound Recorder, or if you are using Windows Vista, Start | Programs | Accessories | Sound Recorder.

Figure 4.5
Windows XP Sound Recorder program.

2. You will now see the Sound Recorder dialog box, as shown in Figure 4.5. If you are using Windows Vista, it will look slightly different but works generally in the same way.

3. Click the red button (or the Start recording button in Vista), and it will begin to record the sound. Speak into the microphone or make a noise.

4. To stop recording, click the black square or the Stop Recording button (Vista).

5. In Windows XP, you will need to do File | Save As to save it in a folder, whereas Vista will automatically ask you for a location to save the file once you stop recording.

Creating Music

When you start creating music for a game, you usually begin with a basic understanding of the type of music you need. For instance, if you are creating music for a wrestling game, classical music is not going to work with that particular genre. You may need to do some research. Discuss the requirements with someone, or find a way to listen to existing music that fits your needs. For a wrestling game, you might watch wrestling on television or attend a wrestling match to get a better understanding of the kind of music users would expect.

If you are writing music for a game that re-enacts the Civil War, you might watch movies about the Civil War or talk with music historians about the types of instruments or music popular during that time period.

It's important to understand that you're not looking to simply copy the music, but to discover what makes music appropriate for the time or era. Keep an open mind. You might base your music on what you've seen and heard, or you may come up with unique ideas.

Programs To Use

There are a number of programs on the market you can consider using. ACID and eJay, for example, use sound loops, which you can place onto the application and arrange any way you choose. Both programs include samples you can use in your musical creations, and you can download clips from several Web sites. Check out *www.sonycreativesoftware.com/products/acidfamily.asp* for more information about ACID and *www.ejay.com* for eJay Dance Studio. eJay Dance 7 is used primarily for making dance music and may not be appropriate if you are trying to make medieval music, for example.

Using Loops

ACID and eJay give you the capability to create music from loops, much like mainstream music is produced today. In the past 20 years, the majority of the music industry has used loops or samples in one way or another. This has drastically altered the musical landscape, changing the way both amateur and professional producers create their music. A quick glance at many modern albums makes it clear that they use loops. The use of samples in many forms of music has brought about an entire industry that produces music, especially for this purpose. Thousands of CDs are available that contain samples you can use for almost any purpose, in standard CD Audio format and in the file formats used by many leading music programs, including ACID and eJay.

Many of these CDs require that you pay for using their samples. There are two basic methods. The first is a royalty-based system, in which the CDs themselves may be free. However, you pay a royalty each time the sample is used. In the second method, you pay an up-front fee, which gives you a royalty-free license that allows you to do almost anything with the loops from that point on. However, with either method, you usually cannot distribute the materials as a new collection of loops. The Internet offers a third way to obtain samples. Many Web sites offer fee-based downloads, while others allow you to download their loops for free. Do a search on Google or go to the relevant product Web sites you might want to use, such as *eJay.com* or *ACIDplanet.com*.

Chapter Summary

It's easy to see why music and sound effects are so important to the development of a game. They can add so much to the experience of a game player by setting a mood or location. Well thought-out music and sound effects go hand in hand with graphics to make the gameplay experience more enjoyable. In the next chapter, we will take a quick tour of the program we are going to use to make our games—the Games Factory 2.

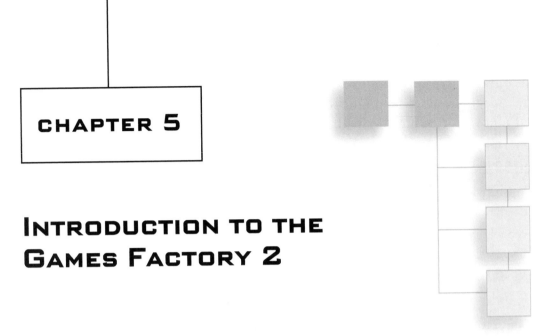

CHAPTER 5

INTRODUCTION TO THE GAMES FACTORY 2

In this chapter:

- What Is TGF2

- TGF2 Installation Requirements

- Installing TGF2

- Starting TGF2 for the First Time

- A Quick Introduction to TGF2

- Chapter Summary

In the following chapters, you will be making a number of games step-by-step using one of the easiest and probably the most powerful 2D game-making program, called the Games Factory 2.

Games Factory 2 Naming Convention

The Games Factory 2 software is also called TGF2 for short, and I've stuck with calling it that from this point forward.

Many of the ideas and techniques you will learn in the games you create for TGF2 in this book will help you make more complex programs using the same process. Once you are comfortable with TGF2, you will be able to use it to produce games and interactive applications with ease. TGF2 also contains state-of-the-art animation tools, movement functions, and game-based routines that make it easy to produce your own games with no programming.

Creating Products with TGF2

You can also make slideshows, interactive tests, presentations, and screensavers with TGF2.

We shall start by installing TGF2 and getting familiar with its major functions. The trial version of the product (TGF2Demo.exe) is available on the CD provided with this book. You will find it in the folder called *Demos*.

What Is TGF2?

TGF2 is a tool used to create games without the need for programming. It achieves this by using an event-based system where the "programmer" uses the mouse to select a number of conditions and actions. This is all done using a graphical interface and does not require the need for the programmer to learn key words or programming terms.

This means that the basic concept of making programs in TGF2 is the same, regardless of what you are trying to make. So you can stop making games for a few months and not have any problems picking back up again and starting right where you left off. The reason for this is that the program is based on the concept of editors, and once you understand how to use them, it's very easy to remember how to put your game together. This is unique in the game-programming world, as most programs require the user to type in text or a combination of text and event-based programming. This can cause the programmer headaches if he doesn't have a great memory for remembering the text that has to be typed in to get something to work.

You may think that the exclusion of typing in lots of text (traditional programming) would mean TGF2 is not very powerful. But TGF2 is a program with a long heritage, and previous versions of it (under other names) have been in existence for over a decade. Over the years, the program has become very powerful and very logical to use, as it has been refined and developed. This makes the development of many 2D programs easy without any programming knowledge.

You can find more information, downloads, and tutorials for TGF2 at the Clickteam Web site: *www.clickteam.com.*

TGF2 Installation Requirements

Tables 5.1 and 5.2 list the basic minimum requirements for installing and running TGF2, as well as the recommended requirements. When possible, you should ensure that you meet or exceed the recommended requirements, as this will lead to a better development experience when working on more complex and resource-hungry games. TGF2 runs on most PC-based configurations and even works on older operating systems, as well as the latest from Microsoft, including Windows Vista.

Table 5.1 Minimum System Requirements for Installing and Running TGF2

Minimum Requirements

Operating system: Windows 95 with IE 4.0, Windows 98, Windows NT 4.0 with Service Pack 3 or
   above, Windows 2000, Windows XP, Windows Vista

Pentium Processor

32 MB RAM with Windows 9x, 64 MB with Windows NT, 128 MB with 2000 and Windows XP,
   512 MB with Vista

CD-ROM drive

Graphics card with 8 MB or more (or minimum OS requirements)

Sound card (optional but recommended)

50–100 MB free hard disk space

Table 5.2 Recommended System Requirements for Installing and Running TGF2

Recommended Requirements

Operating system: Windows 98, Windows 2000, Windows XP, Windows Vista

Pentium 4 Processor

64 MB RAM with Windows 98, 256 MB with Windows 2000 or XP, and 1 GB with
   Windows Vista

CD-ROM drive

Graphics card with 32 MB RAM

Sound card

200–500 MB free hard disk space

Installing TGF2

This section will guide you through the installation of the trial version of TGF2 that is provided on the CD with this book. The TGF2 software is located on the CD in the folder called *Demos*. Find this folder and then double left-click the file TGF2Demo.exe.

1. The first screen you will see is the Welcome dialog shown in Figure 5.1.

   This dialog box gives some details about TGF2 and asks you to ensure that you are not running any other Windows programs before proceeding with the installation.

2. Click the Next button to continue with the installation.

3. The next dialog box provides detailed information about the demo version of the software and what's possible in this version.

4. Read through the information and click Next.

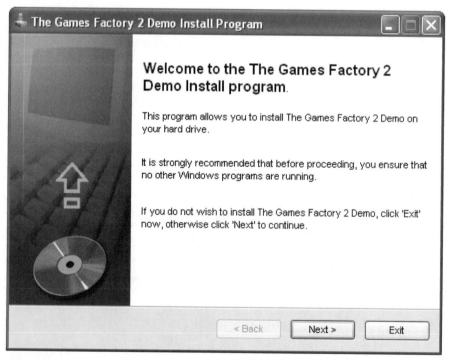

Figure 5.1
TGF2 Welcome dialog box.

5. You will now see the License dialog box. This provides details on what restrictions are placed on using the software and other legal details. To continue, you need to select the I Agree with the Above Terms and Conditions radio button and click Next.

6. Now you will be asked where you want to install the TGF2 files. The default location is C:\Program Files\The Games Factory 2.

   You can either use this path or change it by clicking the button on the right of the path (three dots) within it. Once you have a location you are happy with, click the Next button.

7. You may be advised that the destination folder does not exist and asked if you want to create it. Click Yes to continue.

8. You will now receive a final confirmation message, advising you that the program is ready to copy files to your machine. Click Start to begin the installation of TGF2.

9. After the files have been installed, the final installation dialog box will appear, advising you of the installation success.

10. From this dialog box, you can view the latest product information and visit the support forums. Click the links to access the relevant Web pages or click the Exit button to close the dialog box and complete the installation.

Starting TGF2 for the First Time

When you double left-click the TGF2 icon on the desktop or access it through the Start button, you will be presented with the Demo Version dialog box shown in Figure 5.2. This details what options are missing from the trial version.

The demo version allows you to create games in the TGF2 native format, which can be opened in the full version if you decide to purchase it. You can click the link on the bottom left to visit the Clickteam Web site at *www.clickteam.com* or click Continue to load the program.

Once you have clicked Continue, the TGF2 window appears with a tutorial Help file, as shown in Figure 5.3. This tutorial provides an excellent introduction to the product, and you should consider looking at it after you have read through this chapter. You can close it by clicking the red × in the right-hand corner of the window. If you need to open it again later, select Help | Tutorial.

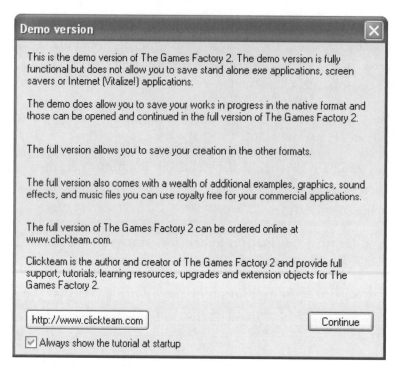

Figure 5.2
The Demo Version information box.

A Quick Introduction to TGF2

TGF2 has three editing screens that allow you to control the main parts of your game:

- **Storyboard Editor**: You can specify the order of the levels in the game.

- **Frame Editor**: You can specify which characters, backgrounds, and objects to put in your level.

- **Event Editor**: You can assign the actions and responses that will make your game come alive.

You can easily move from one editor screen to the next by clicking the Editor icons from the toolbar at the top of the screen. If you are unsure which icon allows you to navigate to which editor, leave your mouse over the icon, and a handy tip message will appear. You can see the icons that allow you to move to the main editors in Figure 5.4.

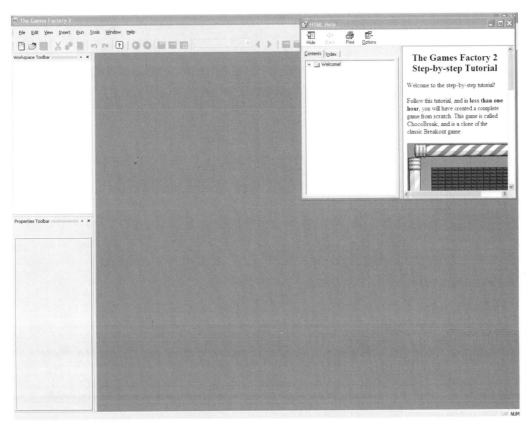

Figure 5.3
The TGF2 program with ChocoBreak tutorial.

Figure 5.4
Storyboard Editor, Frame Editor, and Event Editor.

Storyboard Editor

Most games are composed of several levels. This screen lets you add levels to your game, copy them, and change the order of the levels. This is also where you decide on the size of your playing area, add and edit professional-looking fades in each level, and assign a password to enter each level. You can see a single-level frame shown in the Storyboard Editor in Figure 5.5.

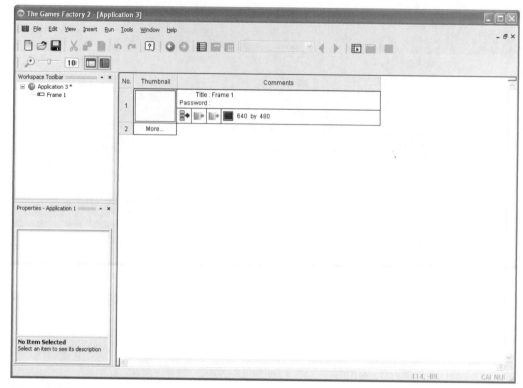

Figure 5.5
Storyboard Editor.

Levels

In TGF2 each separate level or screen is called a *frame*.

Creating a Single Frame Automatically

When you create a new application in TGF2, it will create a single frame (level) automatically.

Frame Editor

The Frame Editor shown in Figure 5.6 is the initial "blank page" for each of your levels. The Frame Editor is where you enter the backdrop objects and the main characters of your game. The white area is where any items are automatically displayed within your games window, and the gray area is out of frame, which allows you to position items that can come into play at a particular moment.

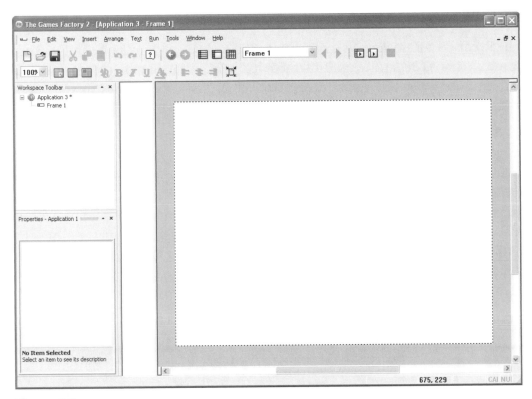

Figure 5.6
The Frame Editor, where you place all your items.

This screen also allows you to access the various libraries that come bundled with the trial and the full version and drop them onto your game. It lets you create your own animated objects, text, and other object types. You could consider the Frame Editor to be the place where you set your scene for your game and prepare and configure any items you have added that are then ready for programming in the Event Editor.

Libraries

A Library is a collection of graphics that you store in a single file, which you can gain access to at any point via the Library Toolbar. You can then drag and drop these objects from the Library quickly and easily into your frame.

Event Editor

The Event Editor is where you begin to build the logic of your game and make it come to life. You create the interactivity here by assigning conditions and actions. When you are experienced with TGF2, you'll spend a lot of your time here. This is the editor where you will program your game.

As shown in Figure 5.7, the Event Editor is set up like a spreadsheet (you can only see the top "spreadsheet row" in the figure example). By filling in the rows and columns, you can assign relationships to each object in your game. This setup makes game building easy, since you can see what happens in your game. Examples of the game-play elements you can build here include aliens colliding with a spaceship, the main character collecting a power-up or getting hit by a missile, setting a time limit, and assigning a sound event. You can create an explosion, destroy an object, add to the score, subtract a life, or specify complicated events, such as changing the direction of a character or a randomly moving object.

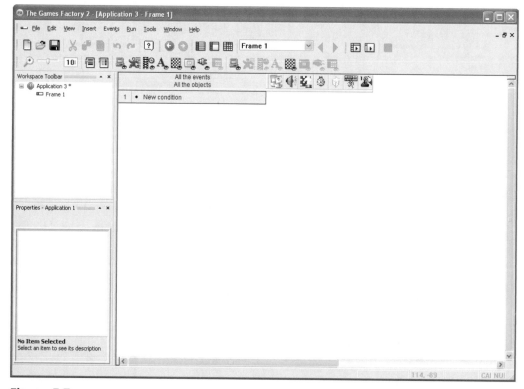

Figure 5.7
The blank Event Editor.

Chapter Summary

That was a quick tour of TGF2. You saw that a game is built in TGF2 in three stages. First, you lay out the flow of your game in the Storyboard Editor. Then you lay out each level and their objects in the Frame Editor. Finally, you use the Event Editor to assign relationships and behaviors to your objects. In the next chapter, you will get to look at a game within the different editors to see how it is made.

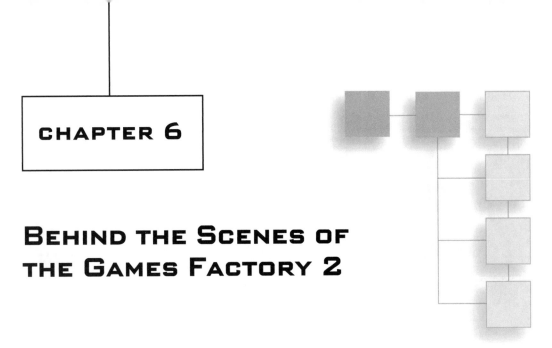

CHAPTER 6

Behind the Scenes of the Games Factory 2

In this chapter:

- About the First Game

- Loading Future Tennis

- Future Tennis: The Storyboard Editor

- Future Tennis: The Frame Editor

- Future Tennis: The Event Editor

- Chapter Summary

The next two chapters will take you through the step-by-step process of creating your first game with TGF2. The game you are going to make is a take on the retro bat and ball game classics that were available on some of the earlier computer game systems. The bat and ball game is still popular today and is a good starting point in learning how to use the product.

Retro Gaming

Retro gaming is very popular. You can still play many classic games such as Pac-Man, Asteroids, and Space Invaders online, purchase them for many different formats or consoles, or if you own a Wii or Xbox, on their respective arcade systems.

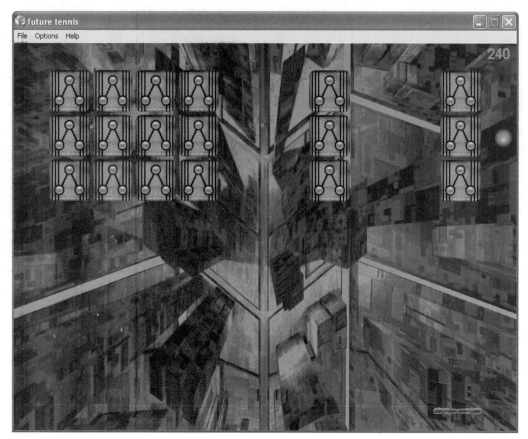

Figure 6.1
The Future Tennis game screen.

About the First Game

Before we begin going through the various editors and options available to you in this game, we need to give you some background on the game. This background explains what the game is about in a simple paragraph.

Story Making

When you are making your own games, it is a good idea to make a story for the game before you start.

The year is 3025 and all sports have been replaced by a single sport called Future Tennis (see Figure 6.1). The event is held once a year and anyone is allowed to enter, but only one player can leave—the winner! Each player enters the Dome to take part in destroying as many blocks as he can. The player who destroys the most blocks is declared the winner. The stakes are high, but the rewards are great—the winner takes the prize fund of one billion credits. Enter the Dome and see if you can take Earth's biggest prize.

Future Tennis will show you the basics of creating games with TGF2. It will show you many of the features and procedures that you will need to follow when making your own games. The great thing about TGF2 is that there are only a handful of editors and screens that you need to work in, so it shouldn't take you too long to get used to the product.

Future Tennis is a straightforward game, and it will introduce you to a number of useful techniques, including the following:

- Moving between screens

- Looping music

- Creating levels

- Moving the mouse

- Assigning buttons on the keyboard to make various things happen within the game

- Creating and using a high-score table

The game is split into three screens (called *frames*): the games menu, the game itself where the player will play Future Tennis, and the third frame, which will display the current high scores.

Loading Future Tennis

The CD-ROM that is provided with this book includes the finished Future Tennis game. In this chapter, we will be loading the game from the CD-ROM and reviewing the code. Here are the steps to get started:

Read-Only CD

As you are loading the game directly from the CD-ROM, you can only review the program (the file will open in read-only format). If you want to make changes to it at a later stage, you need to copy it to your hard disk and then open that copied file.

1. Start TGF2 and click File | Open from the menu.

2. Navigate to your CD-ROM drive and then to the folder Game 1.

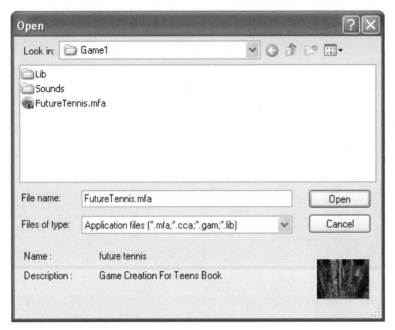

Figure 6.2
Opening the FutureTennis.mfa file.

3. Within this folder, you will see a file called FutureTennis.mfa; single left-click it to select it.

4. In the lower right-hand corner of the dialog box, a small picture appears; this gives you an idea of what the file that you are loading looks like (see Figure 6.2). This feature is particularly useful when you have lots of game files and are looking for a specific example.

5. Click the Open button. This will load the file into TGF2.

Future Tennis: The Storyboard Editor

Now that Future Tennis has been loaded, click the Storyboard icon in the toolbar, and you will see the Storyboard Editor screen (see Figure 6.3).

Starting from the top of the editor screen, let's look at the features of the Storyboard Editor, shown in Figure 6.4. First, look at the number column, which in this example has three boxes with information contained in those rows. These are frame numbers, and frames are the levels or separate screens in our game. Clicking the number will take you directly to that frame and display it in

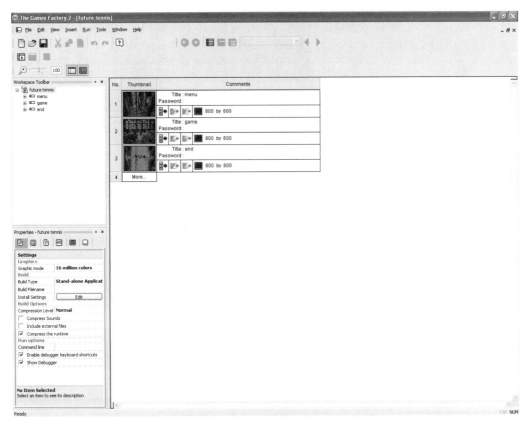

Figure 6.3
The Future Tennis game, as shown in the Storyboard Editor.

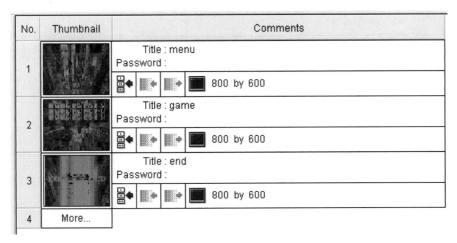

Figure 6.4
Close-up of the Storyboard Editor window.

the Frame Editor. Next to each of these numbers is a small thumbnail picture of the frame of the game. In a large game, this can be useful to help you remember which screen does what, so you don't need to click different frames to find the right one.

Next to the thumbnail images are the comments for that frame, the title of the frame, and the password. To change these, simply left-click the text you want to change. You can edit or add a title or password.

Underneath the comments are several buttons shown in Figures 6.5–6.7. The first button denotes a multimedia frame, which is what all your frames are by default. You can ignore this button, as it has no current function in TGF2. The next button allows you to add a fade-in transition to your frame by using the icon in Figure 6.5. You can add a fade-out transition to your level using the icon in Figure 6.6. If you create a fade-in or fade-out transition, it will appear between the number rows and is then selectable and can be changed or removed if needed.

The play area can be much larger than the screen size, allowing you to create large scrolling games. You can click the monitor to access a drop-down box or click the screen size numbers and type in an exact size. The drop-down screen sizes are shown in Figure 6.7.

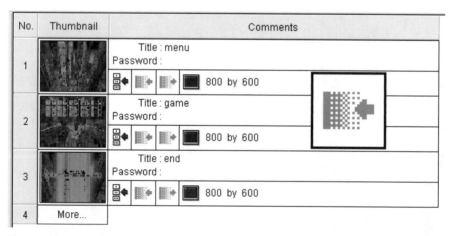

Figure 6.5
The fade-in transition button.

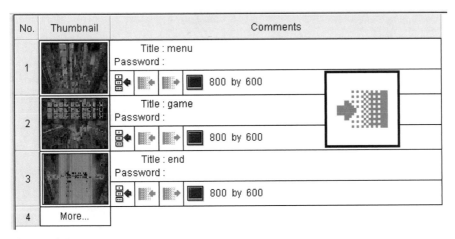

Figure 6.6
The fade-out transition button.

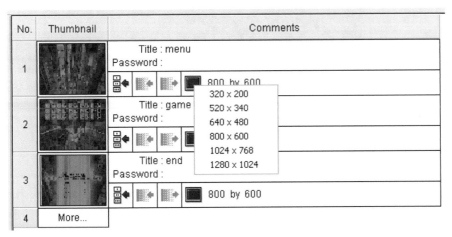

Figure 6.7
The screen size options.

Future Tennis: The Frame Editor

Now let's take a closer look at one of the frames. You could select any of the three frames within your game, but since most of the work needed is on the second frame, click the number 2 in the Storyboard Editor. You can also double left-click the text "game" in the Workspace Toolbar in the left-hand window pane to view the Frame Editor for frame 2.

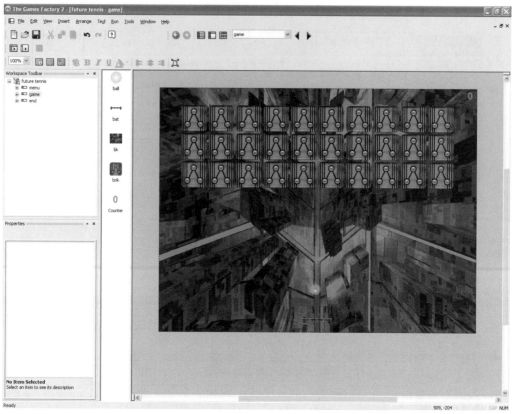

Figure 6.8
The second frame of your Future Tennis game.

When you load frame 2 of the game, you will see various items displayed on the screen, as shown in Figure 6.8.

New Frames

If you are creating a new frame, it will be displayed as a blank white box surrounded by a gray background, since no content has been placed on it yet.

On the left-hand side of the Frame Editor is a group of items displayed in a top-down box. These are the game items that are used within this frame. These items appear when you have added the objects onto the frame. We will go into more detail about what object we are using and how it works in the next chapter.

In the middle of the frame is a scene of a futuristic tennis court and a bat, ball, and some blocks. This is what will be displayed when the user plays the game. The gray around it is outside the play area and is used to place items that won't initially appear in the game or that you will make move into the play area while the game is running.

When there are many objects in a level, not all of them will be placed inside the window, so there is a scroll bar on the bottom-right corner to allow you to move around the Frame Editor area.

When you move your mouse over any of the objects in the frame, a handy hint appears, telling you the name of the item. This is very useful for identifying the name of the object. You may need to use this function when switching between the Frame Editor and the Event Editor. Try dragging a few objects from the level panel and placing them on the screen. As you do so, notice that the Properties window on the left-hand side is then filled with information. You can then use the Object Properties window to configure certain aspects of your objects, for example, their movement, visibility, size, and location on-screen. Make sure not to save the program, as you are just getting used to the various options. If you left-click an object on the frame, you will be able to move it pixel by pixel for perfect placement using the arrow keys. You can also right-click the object and access a pop-up menu that provides additional features and properties. You can see this pop-up menu in Figure 6.9.

Now that you've had a look at some of the items that make up your game, it's a good idea to familiarize yourself with how it plays, as this will ensure that you understand how it all fits together. There are two ways of playing the game. You can either tell TGF2 to play the current frame (frame 2) or play the whole game from the start. Run the whole program so that you experience the whole game. You can see the Run Application and Run Frame icons in the toolbar in Figure 6.10.

Click the Run Application button and play the game. The control for the game is the mouse; move it left and right to move the on-screen paddle. When you have completed playing, you can press the Escape key (the key that says ESC) to exit the game.

Future Tennis: The Event Editor

To get to the Event Editor, click the icon in the toolbar, as shown in the previous chapter. You will see a screen that looks like Figure 6.11. The Event Editor is where you will specify what happens in your game. Some of the things you will be doing for this game include the following:

- Checking for the mouse clicking over a graphic

- Telling the program to move between frames

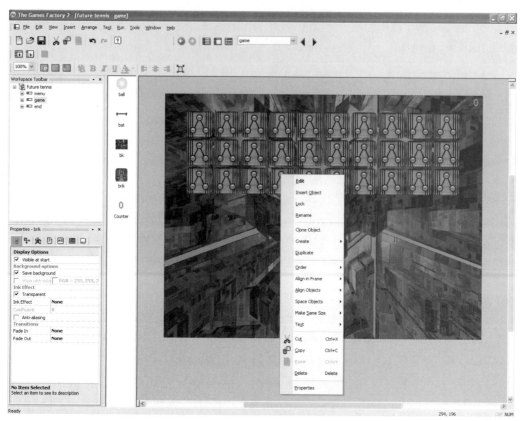

Figure 6.9
The pop-up menu displayed when you right-click an object.

Figure 6.10
The Run Application and Run Frame buttons.

- Creating the code to stop the ball from leaving the screen

- Adding and looping sound

The first time you call up the Event Editor, it will consist of one horizontal line. It looks like a spreadsheet before you have entered any information. Figure 6.11 shows the Future Tennis game with a number of events that have already been

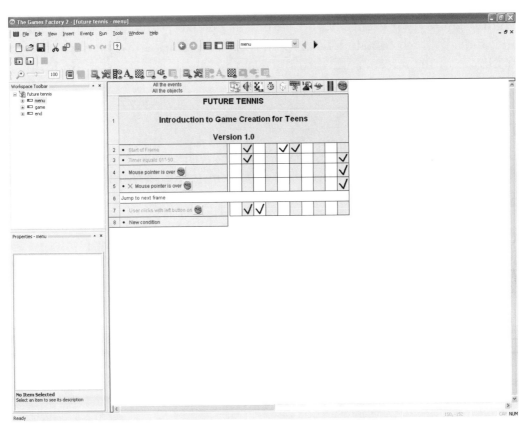

Figure 6.11
The Future Tennis Event Editor.

Figure 6.12
Objects in the Event Editor.

entered. You will have different sets of events for each of the three frames of the game, as each set of events corresponds to that particular frame.

At the top of the Event Editor is a row of icons that represent the possible actions that can happen in your game. A blank game has seven icons that always appear by default. Any icons displayed after this are the objects (graphics and so on) that have been added to the game. Figure 6.12 shows the objects in this game.

To the right of these event lines are a number of boxes, some of which are blank and some of which contain a tick graphic. Each box lines up with an object icon at the top of the screen, and when the event is true, it runs that action for that particular object.

The Object Icons

The first seven icons denote system objects and will appear in every game you create, regardless of whether there are any events or objects within it. The following list shows them in order, as shown in Figure 6.12.

- **Special Conditions**: Performs special functions such as enabling and disabling groups, accessing the clipboard, or accessing text or number variables.

- **Sound**: Plays music or sample files and allows you to pause, play, stop, or select a specific channel on which to play the sound.

- **Storyboard Controls**: Allows you to handle restarting the game, ending the game, and moving between the frames in your game.

- **Timer**: Sets up a timer.

- **Create New Objects**: Allows you to place or create a new object on the screen at certain times or as the result of certain events.

- **Mouse Pointer and Keyboard**: Lets you control how the player interacts with the mouse and keyboard and read key presses or mouse movements.

- **Player 1**: Allows you to change the score and lives of the player.

As previously mentioned, the icons shown after the initial seven are objects that have been added to the actual game. The options for these objects vary depending on what the object does. Additional information on objects is covered in detail in Chapter 10.

The Events

In the Event Editor, each line is given a number. In the first frame, the first line is a comment line, which is used to document certain aspects of your game. In this case, it is a simple version control note, explaining the name of the game and

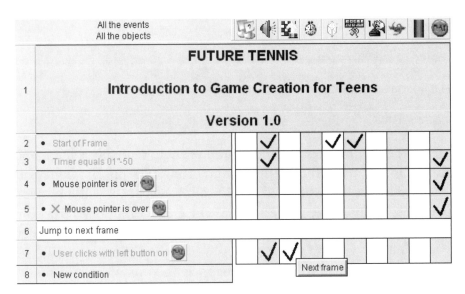

1	**FUTURE TENNIS** **Introduction to Game Creation for Teens** **Version 1.0**									
2	• Start of Frame	✓			✓	✓				
3	• Timer equals 01"-50	✓								✓
4	• Mouse pointer is over									✓
5	• ✗ Mouse pointer is over									✓
6	Jump to next frame									
7	• User clicks with left button on	✓	✓							
8	• New condition									

Figure 6.13
The actions that are contained in the event.

what version it is. You could also put a copyright notice or a helpful note to explain a difficult bit of code.

Most of the events, which are shown in gray, are readable, and you can get an idea of what they do. Event line 2 shows the event Start of Frame. This line and its actions run when the frame is first loaded. Once it has loaded, it will never run this line again until the frame is restarted. Line 7 checks for when the left mouse button has clicked on a specific object. When the event is true (it has been clicked), it will run the actions, which will play a sound and move to the next frame.

You can see what actions will run when an event is true by moving your mouse to an action box, which contains a tick graphic, and it will appear, as shown in Figure 6.13.

Each line is called an event, but within each event you can place multiple conditions. A condition is what you want to check for within your game. For example, look for these conditions:

- Object is moving.

- Object is not moving.

- Sound is playing.

- Mouse enters a certain area on the screen.

- Player has lost all his lives.

- Score reaches 100.

The conditions can get quite complex, but it is important to remember that if one of the conditions is not true, the event will not run, and the program will continue to the next. Once it has finished reading all the events, it will start back from the top and begin the whole process again. Once the condition is true, the program will run the actions (see Figure 6.13). These actions are run in the order in which they were placed, and not in the order in which the objects appear in the Event Editor. Actions are what you want to happen in your game and might include the following:

- Add to score.

- Play a song.

- End the game.

- Place a message on the screen.

Events, Conditions, and Actions

Each frame has its own set of actions and events. You can, of course, have exactly the same events and actions in each frame, but each is a separate entity and is only run when that particular frame is running. Some frames may have many events, while some may only need one; this will all depend on what you are trying to achieve.

Adding to the Event Editor

When you enter events into the Event Editor for the first time, you have a single blank event line. Make sure that you have TGF2 open and click the New button or click File | New to create a new application. You need to be in the blank Event Editor for the first frame that has been created by default. Double left-click the text "Frame 1" in the Workspace Toolbar and then click the Event Editor icon. You are now ready to follow the examples, which give you a quick overview of how to add events, conditions, and actions to your code.

A Comment Line

Comment lines are a great way of putting small bits of information into your game. This allows you to put in your copyright messages or put in notes about a particular bit of code. The second option is very useful if you are working on a difficult bit of code and you want to understand why you did something a particular way when you come back to the code after a break.

To add a comment line you will need to do the following:

1. Right-click the event line number; in a new application or frame that has no events, it will be (1).

2. Select Insert | A Comment. The comment box will appear as shown in Figure 6.14.

3. Type in the comment, and if you want, you can change the font, color, and background color. The color and font have no bearing on the running of any games that you make; these text options only make it easier for the game creator to see his comments in the Event Editor.

4. Click OK to close the dialog box and save its contents to the Event Editor.

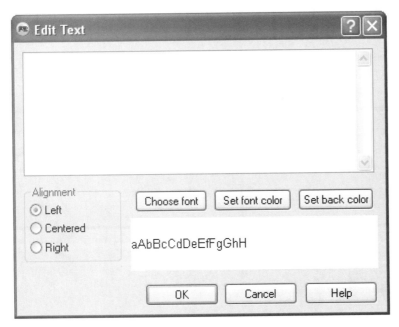

Figure 6.14
The Enter a Comment box.

A Single Condition

If you are adding a single condition to the Event Editor, you can click the New Condition text. The New Condition option exists at the end of the events and at the bottom of all groups of code. (We will discuss groups shortly, but they allow you to put specific code in one block.) This is very useful when you are adding an event to the last line of that set of events.

Events and Conditions

An event is a placeholder for a condition or conditions. Within TGF2, you can have a single condition in an event line, or many conditions.

You may want to insert an event in the middle of some already created code events; if so, you would use the Add a New Event option. When using this option, the event line will appear above the line that is selected.

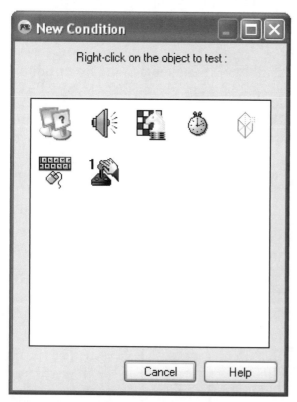

Figure 6.15
The New Condition dialog box.

Using the New Condition Option

If you want to add an event to the very last line of your code (or if there are no events yet, it will be the first line of the program), then left-click New Condition.

A New Condition dialog box will appear with a number of icons, as shown in Figure 6.15. These icons represent the seven default objects and any additional objects that you have added to your game. Each of these objects has a set of conditions from which you can select. Remember, a condition is a "check" that the computer will make to see if something has happened. Now, let's create a Start of Frame condition that will run once when the program runs.

The Start of Frame condition is a Storyboard condition, so right-click the Storyboard icon (it looks like a horse and a chessboard), and you will see a pop-up menu appear. These are the options for which this object can create conditions. Figure 6.16 shows this pop-up menu.

Figure 6.16
The Storyboard icon's conditions.

Objects and Conditions

Each object has a set of conditions that you can select. Different objects have different amounts of options when you click them; some may have many that you can select, while others may only have one or two. If an object doesn't have the condition you are looking for, think about another way of achieving what you are trying to do, because you might be selecting the wrong object.

Select Start of Frame. You now have your first condition in an event block.

Add Another Condition

If you want to create an event with a number of conditions within it, you cannot click New Condition, as this will create a separate event line.

If you still have a single event and a single condition on your screen, right-click the Start of Frame text, which should be in event line number 2 if you added a comment line. (If you do not still have an event and a condition on your screen, follow the details in the last section to remedy this.)

1. From the pop-up menu, select Insert.

2. The New Condition dialog box will appear, allowing you to pick another condition.

3. Select any object and add any condition.

Create a Code Group

Code groups are very useful for putting a selection of code that does a particular job all in one place. This makes your code easier to read, but you can also enable and disable code groups at any time, which means that you can turn on and off particular code when necessary.

To add a group:

1. Right-click any event number and select Insert | A Group of Events.

2. A Group Events dialog box will appear as shown in Figure 6.17.

Then you will need to:

■ Type in the title of the group.

■ You can type in a password if you want to protect the group and prevent someone from opening the group if you distribute your code.

Figure 6.17
A blank code group ready to be created.

2	**First Group**
3	• New condition

Figure 6.18
An example of a group that has been created.

- By default, the group is active when the program or frame is running, but if you want it to run only at a specific time, you can unselect this box and enable the group through an action.

- Once you are done, click OK. Your group is now created and looks something like Figure 6.18.

Adding an Action

To add an action, you need to move to the right of the event line to which you want to add the action. Consider what action you want to implement, and in all cases, it will be specific to a particular object or contained within the seven system objects.

Taking Action

An action is what you want to happen on the screen, when a specific condition(s) is true.

For example, consider for a moment that you have created a bat and ball game in which the ball hits a number of bricks and the player has a bat and tries to keep the ball in play. You have just created a condition that checks for when the ball hits the bat. When you run the game, nothing happens when the ball hits the bat, as you haven't created the action. Therefore, the action you want to apply is to make the ball bounce. Because you are going to tell the ball to bounce, you move directly under the ball object and apply a bounce to it. You will apply all of your actions in TGF2 by using this same logic.

To add an action, move to the correct event line where you want to place an action and then move under the object to which you want to apply the action. Right-click the white box to reveal a pop-up menu. An example of the actions under the Storyboard Control object is shown in Figure 6.19.

Select any action from the pop-up menu, and this will place a tick graphic in the box. This tells you there is an action within this location. If you want to add a second action to the same event line and the same object, you can right-click again and select the action.

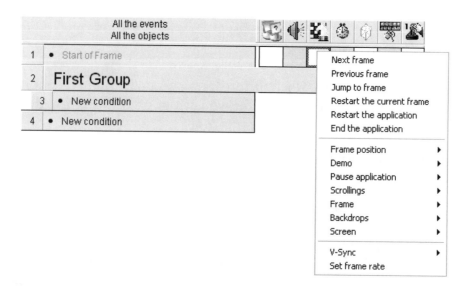

Figure 6.19
The actions menu available to the Storyboard Control object.

Chapter Summary

This chapter looked at the game you will be making in the next chapter called Future Tennis. You will build your game frame by frame, and by the end, you should have a pretty good idea of how to use TGF2 and how to program in the Event Editor. We have covered a lot of information in the last few chapters, so don't be afraid to go back and re-read anything you are not sure about. By making the game in the next chapter, you will begin to get an idea of how conditions and actions work. When game-making, you will find that it is all very logical. Simply visualize what you think needs to happen in your game and apply this information to the Event Editor. So now let's begin our first game, Future Tennis.

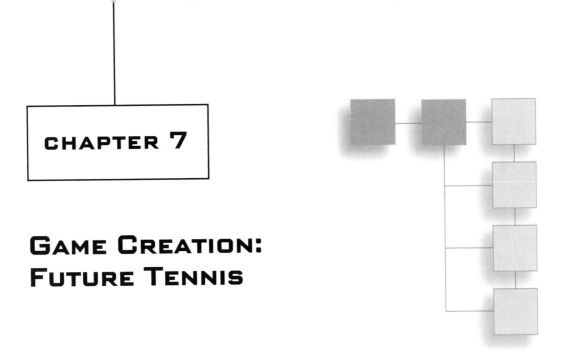

CHAPTER 7

GAME CREATION: FUTURE TENNIS

In this chapter:

- Library and Content

- Initial Setup

- Event Programming

- Additional Notes about the Game

- Chapter Summary

In this chapter, you will be creating a futuristic bat and ball game discussed in Chapter 6. You will need to create your game file, set up your frames and the objects on-screen, program the game to react to the player's key presses, and finally program the game's logic. So let's now begin putting together our game of Future Tennis.

Library and Content

The Library Toolbar is a useful way of adding objects and items already created onto your blank frames. These objects could be the graphical content of your games or game-related objects that have already been configured in TGF2. So you don't have to spend a lot of time drawing the spaceships and backgrounds; this has already been done for you when you create the games in this book.

Before you start, you need to connect to a Library file that contains all of your objects. The Library Toolbar is in the bottom part of the TGF2 screen, as shown in Figure 7.1.

If you do not see the toolbar, you need to display it by selecting View | Toolbars | Library Window.

You now need to connect this Library window to the Library file that has already been created for you. To do this, try the following:

1. Right-click the left windowpane, and a pop-up menu will appear. Select New.

2. A Browse for Folder dialog box allows you to search for the folder that contains the library. Navigate to the CD-ROM provided with this book.

3. Navigate to the Game1\Lib folder and then click OK.

4. You can now type the name of your Library folder, so in the left window-pane where you see the words New Library, type **Future Tennis**.

5. Clicking the words Future Tennis in the left-hand pane will reveal the Library file in the right-hand window, as shown in Figure 7.2.

Figure 7.1
The blank Library Toolbar.

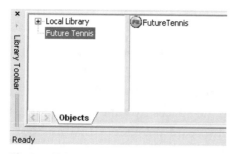

Figure 7.2
The Future Tennis Library file.

Now that you have connected to the Library, you can create your TGF2 file and set up the basics before placing the objects on-screen.

Initial Setup

You need to begin by creating a blank game file and then creating the frames that will represent the screens within the game.

First, you need to create a TGF2 file:

1. Click New or select File | New.

2. Your TGF2 game file will be created, as shown in Figure 7.3.

   Notice that the Storyboard Editor shows that the only frame is set to a size of 640 × 480. The game you are about to create works on an 800 × 600 screen

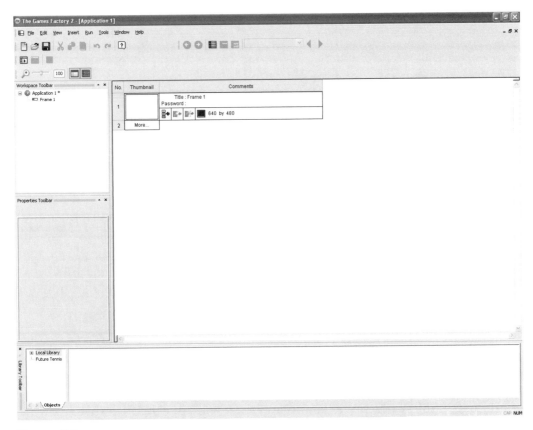

Figure 7.3
The blank game file ready to be configured.

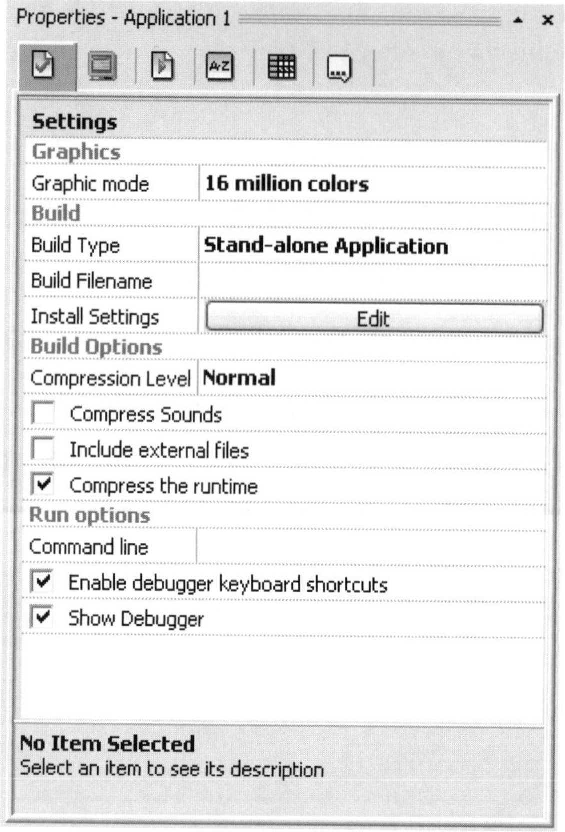

Figure 7.4
The Properties window displaying application information.

resolution. TGF2 has a frame resolution and an application resolution, and changing the application resolution changes the size of the current frame and any additional ones you create.

3. Single left-click Application 1 in the Workspace Toolbar. This reveals the Application Properties information in the Properties Toolbar, as shown in Figure 7.4.

4. At the top of the Properties window in Figure 7.4 are a number of tabs. Click the Windows tab. This is the one that looks like a monitor.

5. The first item in the Properties window is now the Size item, and it is set to 640 × 480. Click the box, and an arrow will appear. Click this arrow and select 800 × 600 from the drop-down menu. Then click anywhere on the frame.

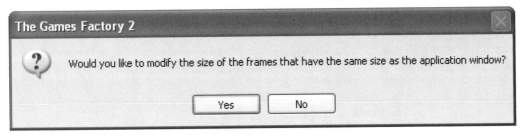

Figure 7.5
Changing all frames to the application size.

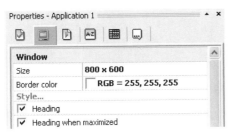

Figure 7.6
The changed Application window size.

6. A dialog box asks if you want to modify the frames to the same as the newly set application size, as shown in Figure 7.5. Click Yes to agree to this.

You can see the changed settings in the Properties - Application 1 window in Figure 7.6.

Properties Window Display

In some cases when you click a dialog box, the Properties window will become blank. To display the correct information, click the object you are interested in. For example, if you were viewing the Application Properties, click the application name in the Workspace Toolbar.

Creating and Renaming Frames

You have three frames in your game, and by default the new program file only has one, so you need to create two more.

1. Right-click the application name and select New Frame (see Figure 7.7). This creates a second frame called Frame 2.

2. Right-click the application name again and select New Frame. This creates a third frame called Frame 3.

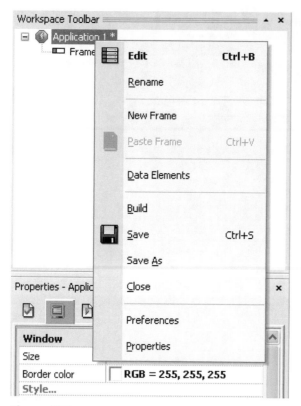

Figure 7.7
The Rename and New Frame options using the right mouse click.

You now have all three frames in place and are ready to rename them so they are easier to identify. This identification is not such a problem in a small game like this, but some games could run to a couple of hundred frames, and at this point it can get very confusing as to what each frame does. It is good to get into the habit of giving your frames identifiable names, as this will be very helpful in larger projects. For example, don't leave a frame just called *Frame,* call it *Level 1,* and so on.

3. Right-click the Frame 1 text and select Rename from the pop-up menu. Type **menu** into the selected text box.

4. Right-click Frame 2, select Rename, and then type **game**.

5. Once more, right-click Frame 3, select Rename, and then type **end**.

You have renamed your frames, but it is also good practice to rename your application. This name is particularly important because when you run

Figure 7.8
The current state of the Workspace Toolbar.

your game in a window, the application name is the name that will appear in the top bar of the window.

6. Right-click Application 1 in the Workspace Toolbar.

7. Select Rename and type **Future Tennis**.

Your Workspace Toolbar should now look like Figure 7.8.

Menu Frame Setup

You now need to place all the objects you are going to use in your game for the menu frame. To do this, you need to ensure that you are on the correct frame and that you have the correct objects for the frame ready to drop into place.

1. In the Library Toolbar, double left-click the Library file Future Tennis.

2. You will now see the names of the frames you are going to use in the game, as shown in Figure 7.9. This Library file is an exact replica of the frames you have and contains the objects for each frame that you need to place.

3. Double left-click menu in the Library Toolbar to display all the available objects (see Figure 7.10).

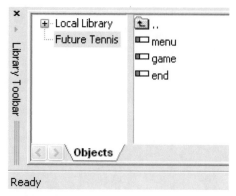

Figure 7.9
Each frame in the Library contains all of the objects you need to create the content for your game.

Figure 7.10
The Library objects for the menu frame.

You are now ready to drag and drop items from the Library onto the frame, but you need to ensure that you are on the Frame Editor for the correct frame, which in this case is the recently renamed frame, menu.

4. Click the number 1 in the Storyboard Editor to access the blank game frame or double left-click the word *menu* in the Application Properties Toolbar.

You now have the blank frame in front of you, ready for you to begin placing items on the screen, as shown in Figure 7.11.

Setting Up the Scene

It's time to create the scene for the main frame by dragging objects from the Library Toolbar and placing them in particular positions.

1. Left-click and hold and drag the object called Backdrop from the Library Toolbar; move it over to the blank frame area. Release the left mouse button to place the object on the screen.

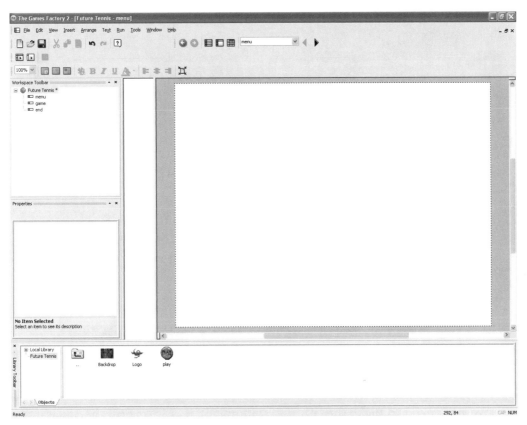

Figure 7.11
The blank menu frame ready for dropping the objects onto.

2. The background graphic will probably not be positioned correctly on the frame, but this doesn't matter, since it's quite easy to move it after it has been placed. After it has been placed on the frame, single left-click the graphic to display the object's properties in the Properties Toolbar.

3. Click the Size/Position tab in the Properties Toolbar (displayed as two arrows appearing from a box).

4. Change the X position to 0 and the Y position to 0. This places the object at the very top left side of the frame, which means it will cover the whole frame because its size is 800 × 600, which is the size of the frame.

X and Y Positions

Remember that X is the position from the top left to the top right, and Y is from the top left to the bottom left.

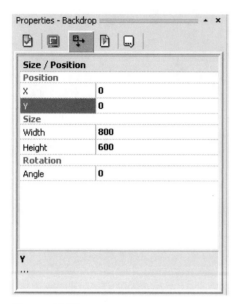

Figure 7.12
The updated position of the backdrop object.

5. This will display the object's current position, as shown in Figure 7.12.

   We now need to place the other two items for this frame on the screen: the Logo and the Play button.

6. Drag and drop the Logo object on the frame.

7. Single left-click the object to access the Object Properties; then click the Size/Position tab and type in **9** for the x-coordinate and **0** for the y-coordinate. This will place the Logo object in the middle of the frame.

8. Drag and drop the Play object onto the frame.

9. Single left-click the object and click the Size/Position tab. Type in the x-coordinate of **360** and the y-coordinate of **600**.

   This will place the object just outside the frame at the bottom. You can see the general position of all three items in Figure 7.13; however, on your frame, you may not have enough space to see the all-in-one go without scrolling the frame.

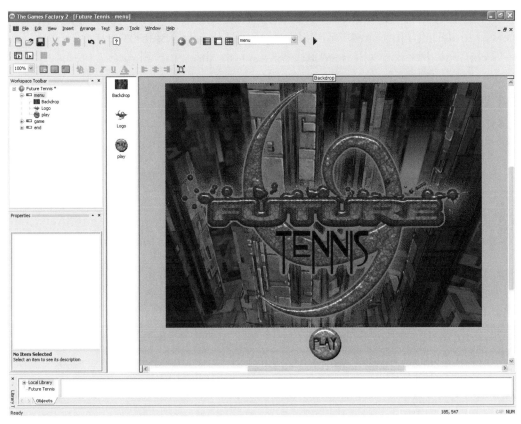

Figure 7.13
The setup of the menu frame.

The Game Frame Setup

You now need to place all the objects you are going to use in the game for the game frame. Make sure that you are on the correct frame. Double left-click the text game in the Workspace Toolbar to display the blank frame.

Changing the Library Folder

Now, you need to change the Library file location, as currently it is pointing to objects that were required for the menu frame.

1. In the Library Toolbar are objects that you dragged onto the frame for the menu frame and a yellow folder graphic with an up-pointing arrow. Double left-click the yellow folder to move back up a level.

2. You can now see the three frame folders, which contain your content. Double left-click the game folder in the Library Toolbar to display the content that you will need to add next, as shown in Figure 7.14.

Setting Up the Scene

It's now time to create the scene for the game frame. Again, you will need to drag objects from the Library Toolbar and place them in particular positions.

1. Drag the object BK from the Library Toolbar and drop it onto the blank frame.

2. Left-click the object to access its properties in the Properties window; then click the Size/Position tab (in the Object Properties window).

3. Change the X position to 0 and the Y position to 0. This will place the item in the top left-hand corner.

    You can now place the rest of the items in the same manner using the coordinates given in Table 7.1.

Now that you have placed all these items, your screen will look like Figure 7.15.

You may notice that you have only one brick on the frame at the moment, which won't be much fun playing this type of game. What you need to do is create a set

Figure 7.14
The game Library items.

Table 7.1 Game Frame Object Positions

Object Name	X	Y
Ball	396	493
Bat	360	558
Brick	57	43
Score	789	26

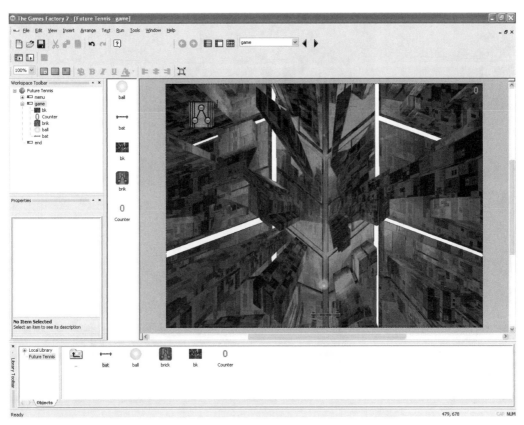

Figure 7.15
The current positions of the objects in the game frame.

of bricks to make the game more fun and challenging. There are a number of ways to do this. For example, you could manually place each brick on the screen. This would be a lot of work and would take some time to precisely place each brick. Alternatively, you could use another method, which allows you to duplicate the brick and get TGF2 to place it at specific points in one go. The second option is easier and a lot quicker.

Before you duplicate (copy) an object, it is good to know how many you think you might need and what space between each item is required. In this case, you will need a total of 10 brick columns and three rows, which gives you a total of 30 bricks.

To duplicate the brick, you need to do the following steps:

1. Right-click the brick object and select Duplicate from the pop-up menu (shown in Figure 7.16).

Figure 7.16
The pop-up menu when right-clicking an object.

2. A dialog box will appear, asking for specific details of where you want to place these new items and how many you want. As previously mentioned, you want 10 columns and 3 rows, so in the Rows box type **3**, Columns **10**. For spacing, sometimes this can be a case of try it and see if it works. I've already tested different combinations, and a row and column spacing of five works well, so enter this into both boxes.

3. Your Duplicate Object dialog box will look like Figure 7.17. Click the OK button to create the objects on the frame. After you have clicked OK, you will see the bricks that have been placed, as in Figure 7.18.

Creating Copies of Objects

When you are placing items on the frame using the Duplicate option, it is useful to remember the Undo option. After you have entered the numbers in the Duplicate dialog, you may find the items are not spread out as well as you hoped. By holding down the CTRL (Control) key and pressing Z, you can undo what has been placed on-screen, allowing you to follow the process again and enter a different set of spacing information.

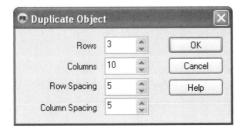

Figure 7.17
The Duplicate dialog box with your settings.

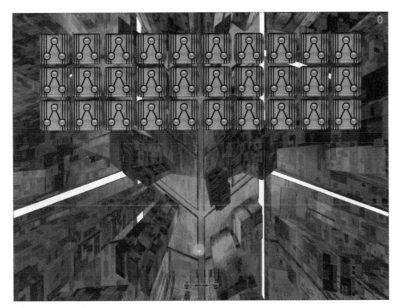

Figure 7.18
The placement of the bricks after duplication.

Changing the Game Background Color

You may have noticed on the background image a number of white streaks, which happens because there is transparency on the image. Transparency means you can see right through parts of the image straight to what's behind it. Unfortunately, at the moment all that is behind this object is a white background. This obviously doesn't look correct because for this game it's meant to be red, so we need to change the background frame color. To do this, we will need to access the frame properties.

1. Click the game text in the Workspace Toolbar to bring up the frame properties.

2. You will see an option called Background Color, and you will notice currently that it is set to white. If you click the small white box, a color palette appears; click the red color box.

3. This will change the background to red, which makes the background now look correct.

End Frame Setup

You now need to place all of the objects you are going to use in the game for the end frame. The end frame will be used to display high scores that have been obtained. To begin, you must make sure you are on the correct frame. Double left-click the text game in the Workspace Toolbar to display the blank frame.

Changing the Library Folder

You will now need to change the Library file location, as currently it is pointing to objects that were required for the menu frame.

1. In the Library Toolbar are objects that you dragged onto the frame for the game frame and a yellow folder graphic with an up-pointing arrow. Double left-click the yellow folder to move back up a level.

2. You can now see the three frame folders, which contain your content. Double left-click the game folder in the Library Toolbar to display the content that you will need to add next, as shown in Figure 7.19.

Setting Up the Scene

It's now time to create the scene for the final frame, called the end frame. We will follow the same process as before and drag and drop the objects onto the frame area.

1. Drag and drop the object called Backdrop onto the frame.

Figure 7.19
The end frame Library items.

2. Left-click the object to access its properties and then click the Size/Position tab.

3. Type in **0** for the x-coordinate and **0** for the y-coordinate.

   You only need one other object for this screen, and this is the high-score table. This object lets you easily check for top scores and display them within a table.

4. Drag and drop the object Hi-Score onto the frame, click the object to access its properties, and then choose the Size/Position tab in the Object Properties window.

5. Set the x-coordinate at 276 and the y-coordinate at 328. Your frame should now look like Figure 7.20.

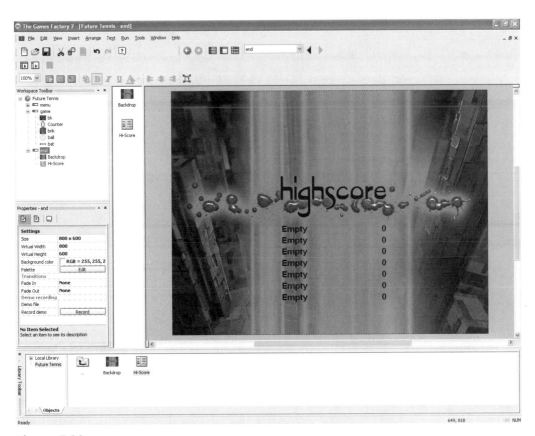

Figure 7.20
The end frame with all the objects in place.

Event Programming

In this section of the book, you'll begin to program the events that bring all the frames together to create your game.

You will work on each frame separately, which makes the process of making your game easier because you can get one frame working before you move on to the next. The major benefit of a frame system is that you can pick and choose which frame to work on first. This means that you can leave difficult bits until later, when you are ready to work on them. As this is a simple game, you will be working on it in the order you created the frames.

Programming the Menu Frame

The menu frame is the first screen that the player is introduced to, and its main goal is to direct the player to the areas of the game that he might want to go to. In Future Tennis, we only have three frames, so we don't have many areas that the player can navigate to. In fact, all that the player can select is to play the game by clicking the Play button once it appears.

Before you start, you need to make sure you are on the correct frame:

1. Double left-click on menu in the Workspace Toolbar.

2. You will see the menu frame with the objects in place, ready for you to begin coding the logic for the game.

   To begin coding, you will need to be in the Event Editor for the current frame, so click the Event Editor button on the toolbar.

Menu Frame Components

In the menu frame, you will want to achieve several things:

- Create a comment line to state the game name, what the game is for, and the current version number.

- At the start of the program, play a song and loop it.

- At 1.5 seconds, play an exploding sound and make the Play button appear at a specific spot.

- Check for when the mouse pointer is over the Play button and make the Play button highlighted.

- Check for when the mouse pointer is not over the Play button and make the Play button go back to its original state.

- Check for when the player clicks the Play button, plays a sound, and then moves to the next frame.

Creating the Note Event

The first bit of event program isn't actually making anything happen on-screen. Let's add a message to the start of the game, detailing the game, what its being made for, and the version number. You can add as much or as little information as you require for your own games. Adding notes is a useful way of telling you what's going on in your program, so if you come back to some code after a long time away you can understand it again quickly.

1. Right-click event number 1 and select Insert | A Comment. The Edit Text dialog box appears.

2. Type **FUTURE TENNIS** and press the Return (Enter) key twice to create a space. Then type **Introduction to Game Creation for Teens**.

3. Press the Return key twice again and then type **Version 1.0**.

4. Click the Centered button to center the text.

   We want to change the background color, its alignment, and the text size. As you can see from the dialog box in Figure 7.21, there are a number of options available for configuring how the comment box looks.

5. Click the Choose Font button to access the font options in Figure 7.22. Ensure that the text style is bold and the size is 14, as shown in Figure 7.22. Click OK to save the changes to the dialog box.

6. Click Set Back Color, and a Color dialog box will appear, allowing you to select a color that you want to display as the background to your comment box. As you can see in Figure 7.23, we have selected a color to use for our comment box. Select the same color and then click OK to close the Color dialog box.

7. You will now be back at the Edit Text dialog box. Click the OK button to save the information to the Event Editor. You will see the event comment in the Event Editor, as shown in Figure 7.24.

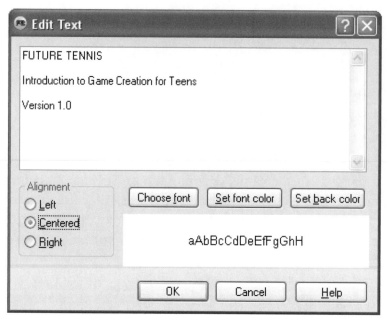

Figure 7.21
The Edit Text dialog box with various option buttons.

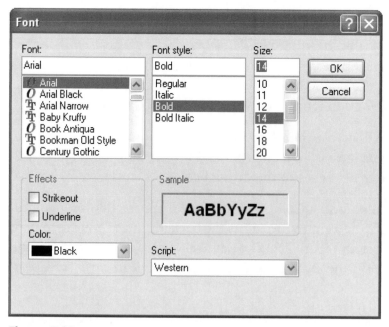

Figure 7.22
The Font dialog box.

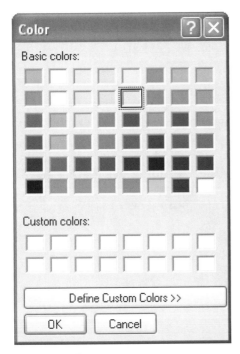

Figure 7.23
The Color Picker with the color selected.

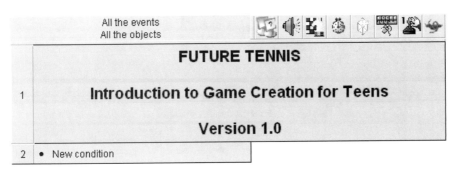

Figure 7.24
The comment displayed in the Event Editor.

Start of Frame Event

At the very start of the frame, we want to play some music. This action will appear in the start of frame event, which means that as soon as the frame appears on-screen, this action will happen.

Let's play some music at the very beginning of the game to create some atmosphere and make it more enjoyable for the player. We will start by adding the event.

1. Click the New Condition text, which appears on event line 2.

2. In the New Condition dialog box, right-click the Storyboard Controls icon (the horse and chessboard icon).

3. From the pop-up menu, select Start of Frame, as shown in Figure 7.25.

4. You will now have a new event on event line 2, and it will read Start of Frame.

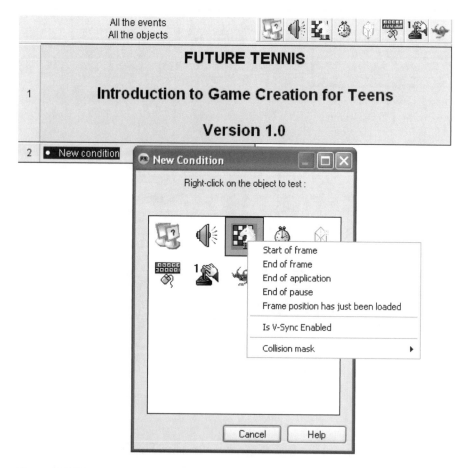

Figure 7.25
Pop-up menu from the Storyboard Controls icon.

This event will occur only at the start of the frame. After the program has run this event, it won't run it again, though any actions that have taken place which last longer than this event will continue to run (for example, playing a sound or music). We now need to create our first action for this event, which will be to play a song.

1. Move to the right of the Start of Frame event, until you are directly under the Sound object (the icon that looks like a speaker).

2. Right-click the blank action box to display the actions available for this object, and then select the Samples option to reveal all options that relate to this menu, as shown in Figure 7.26.

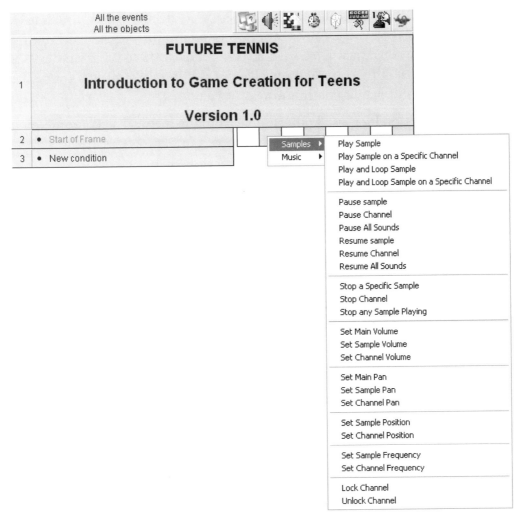

Figure 7.26
Actions for the Sound object Samples menu.

As you can see, the Samples option allows for many different actions and options for sounds. We could just play a single sound file, which in this case is a standard WAV-formatted sound file.

WAV Format

WAV files are a standard file format for sound and music files that are played on the PC. You can create your own sound files using the Windows Sound Recorder and then save them as a WAV-formatted file that will allow you to play them in the Games Factory 2. Alternatively, you could purchase a WAV sounds CD or find free ones on the Internet.

Once it has played, it won't play again (unless we create another event to check when it has finished playing). Another option is to loop the music, which means that once it has finished, it will play again. TGF2 allows you to specify how often you want the music to loop. Alternatively, you can loop it until the frame has been completed and play it continuously.

1. Select the option Play and Loop Sample from the menu. The Play and Loop Sample dialog box will then appear as shown in Figure 7.27.

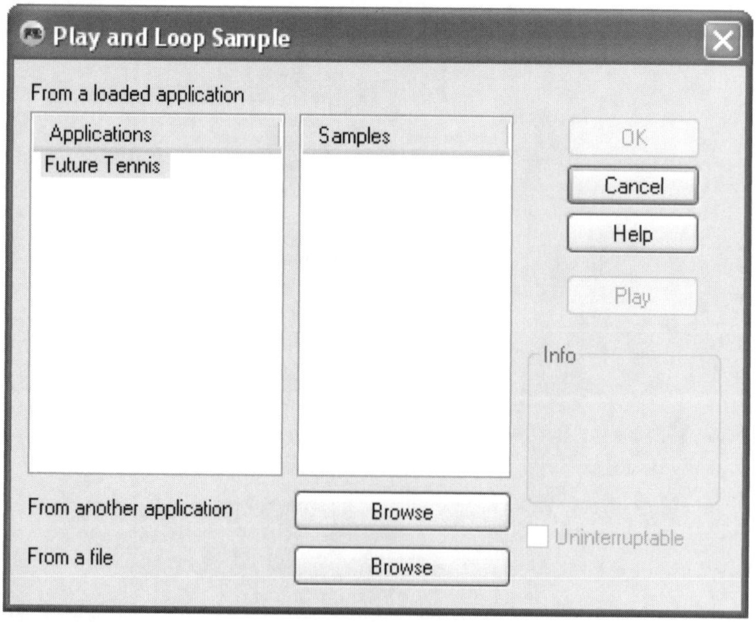

Figure 7.27
The Play and Loop Sample dialog box.

Figure 7.28
The Sounds folder, which contains the file we want to play at the start of the frame.

This allows you to search for sound files on your hard drive or any files contained within another Games Factory file.

2. We want to search for a file that is contained on the CD-ROM that comes with the book. So click the Browse button that is opposite the text: From a File.

3. Browse to your CD-ROM drive and into the Game1\Sounds folder, and you will see the file SpatialMaths.wav. If you single left-click the file, you can click the Play button to hear what it sounds like. This is very useful if you are looking through lots of sound files and want a particular sound to go with your game. You can see the dialog and the file in Figure 7.28.

4. Click the Open button to continue with this sound file.

5. Since we want this sound file to play more than once, an additional dialog box will appear, as shown in Figure 7.29. This asks for how many times

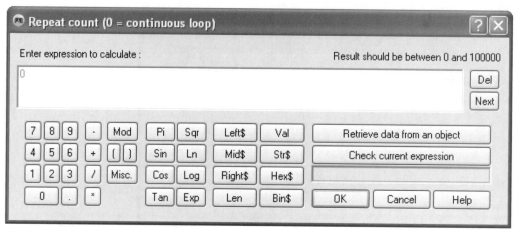

Figure 7.29
Here's the dialog to specify how many times to loop a song.

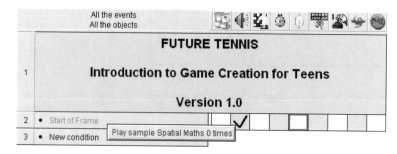

Figure 7.30
The action displayed while holding the mouse cursor over the action.

the sound file should play. If you put in a number of 1 or above, it will play the song that many times; if you put in a 0, then it will play until the frame ends. Replace the 1 with a 0 and then click OK.

If you press F7, this will play the frame, and an application window will appear with the background graphic, the logo will appear, and the game will play the song SpatialMaths.wav. Well done! You have completed your first event and action, and you will be completing your first game in no time at all.

You can see the action you created by holding the mouse over the checked icon; this is very useful if you want to read what is going on in your program, as shown in Figure 7.30.

Timer Event

After one-and-a-half seconds, we will play a sound and display the Play graphic on the screen. The Timer system object handles all timed events. For the graphic to appear, we will be moving it into position, but we could have put it into position to begin with and then changed the properties of the object and made it invisible and then made it visible again when we wanted it to appear. TGF2 is very good at allowing you to program the same effect by using more than one method.

First, let's create the Timer condition:

1. Click the New Condition text on event line 3; then right-click the stopwatch icon, which represents the Timer system object. You will have a number of different Timer conditions that you can pick. We want to do something when the Timer is at a specific time, so select Is the Timer Equal to a Certain Value.

2. A Timer dialog box will appear, which allows you to enter in a set of numbers or use the slider. Copy the dialog shown in Figure 7.31 and then click OK.

3. Move to the right of this new event until you are under the Sound system object; right-click the blank action box to reveal the options.

4. Select the Samples menu option and then Play Sample. The Play Sample dialog box will appear, and you will notice that you can see the Spatial Maths sound that you already added to the game earlier.

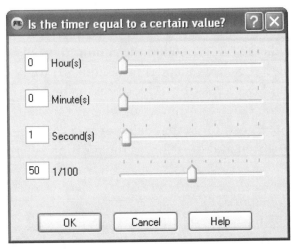

Figure 7.31
The Timer dialog box with the one-and-a-half seconds configured.

5. Click the Browse button opposite the From a File button.

6. The dialog box should now open up in the Sounds folder on the CD-ROM; if not, navigate to the CD-ROM drive containing the CD from this book and then GAME1\Sounds.

7. Select the file called EXPLOD09.wav and click the Open button. This will apply the action to play this sound file.

Press the F7 key to run the frame. You will notice that the program window appears, the Logo zooms in, and music is playing. After one-and-a-half seconds, an exploding sound can be heard.

Now we need to add the action to make the Play button appear on-screen. Currently, it is placed at the screen location of 360 by 600, but before we place the object, we should also create another action to make the Play button appear at the very front of the frame. When you place objects on-screen, they are layered, meaning the first object placed will appear behind the second object placed. This does not include backdrop objects that always appear at the back of any other objects. Sometimes, it's a good idea to force an object to the front if you are unsure of its current layer position.

So let's create the action to place the Play button at the front of any other objects:

1. Move to the right of the event where you added the sound on event line 3, until you are directly under the Play object. Right-click the blank action box and then select the menu option Order | Bring to Front.

2. Now that we have brought the object to the front of the screen, let's set its new position. In the same box where you just added the action to bring the Play object to the front (where the check mark is now situated), right-click and select Choose Position | Select Position. A position dialog box will appear, asking you to enter the exact coordinates of where you want to place the item. You can type the position in manually, or you can see a small box with a cross in it on-screen and drag this to the position where you want to place the object.

Precise Positioning of an Object

When using the box with a cross in it to place the object, remember the box represents the top left-hand corner of the object.

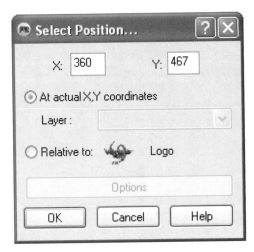

Figure 7.32
Select Position of an Object dialog box.

3. We have already worked out the position where we want the Play button to appear, so type in X as **360** and Y as **467**, as shown in Figure 7.32. Click OK to save this to the Event Editor.

Starting Positions of Objects

When you are creating your scenes, sometimes it's a good idea to place the objects in the positions you want them to appear in the game, make a note of that position, and then move them to their starting positions. This will save you time when working out any positions that you need to change through the life of the game.

You should now have the actions in your event shown in Figure 7.33.

Saving Your Work

As you make your games, you should try to save your work as you progress through the examples. Even though TGF2 is very stable, it is possible that a combination of other programs and your own hardware could cause a crash. It is very upsetting to lose any work that you might have spent time on since you last saved your game, so it is sensible to save your work after every few events.

To save for the first time, click the Save or the Save As button, and you'll be asked for the name of the file that you want to save and the location where it should be saved. After the first save, when you click Save, it will overwrite the original file. Using the Save As option allows you to save the file as a different file name. You can see the Save and Save As options in the File menu (see Figure 7.34).

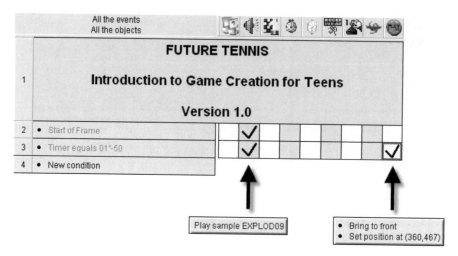

Figure 7.33
The actions assigned to your event.

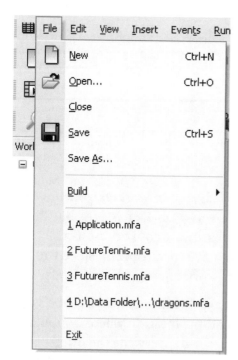

Figure 7.34
The Save and Save As menu options.

Saving Your Games

On a regular basis, use the Save As option and save the file with a different name, which allows you to go back to an earlier file if you need to for any reason. If you overwrite the file, you will only be left with a single file to access, and any corruption or issues of that file will then mean you have lost all of your work.

Mouse Pointer Is Over

Our next event will check to see if the mouse cursor is over the Play object, which is going to be our button to the next frame. When the mouse is over it, then a different animation will be played to show that the object is selected.

Let's start with the condition to check for the position of the mouse. Use the Mouse Pointer and Keyboard system object to do this.

1. Click the New Condition text on event line 4. The New Condition dialog will appear; right-click the Mouse Pointer and Keyboard object (this object looks like a mouse and keyboard).

2. Two menu options appear: one for the mouse and one for the keyboard. Because the condition we are trying to check for is based on the position of the mouse, select the Mouse option.

3. Then choose Check for Mouse Pointer over an Object. A dialog box will now appear (see Figure 7.35), which displays all available objects in this frame that you can test the position of the mouse against. We want to test the mouse when it's over the Play object, so select the Play object and click OK.

Now we need to create the action for this event, which involves changing an animation of an object. An animation is a set of images played quickly to make a graphic look like it is moving, talking, waving, jumping, and so on. Objects that have animations in TGF2 are called *active objects*. This is something we will look at in more detail later in Chapter 10.

TGF2 comes with a default set of animation group names, for example Walking, Stopped, Jumping, Falling, and so on. These default set names are there to help you understand what animations you may need for your objects. You could also create your own animation set names, but it's just as easy to use these free slots. The problem is that you must remember where you placed your images in order to call them from the Event Editor. We will cover animations in more detail in Chapter 11.

Figure 7.35
A selection of objects that you would be able to test against.

For the Play object, we have two animation groups being used: one called Stopped and the other called Walking. In each of the two animation groups, there is a single image—one that is the normal image that you see when placing the object on-screen, and a version that is lighter when the animation is changed to Walking. These two simple color changes to the image will allow you to create the simple effect of highlighting the object when the mouse moves over it.

Let's change the animation from Stopped to Walking, so that it will change the graphic to a lighter color.

1. Move to the right of event line 4 until you are directly under the Play object.

2. Right-click the blank action box and select Animation | Change | Animation Sequence.

3. This will now display an Animation Sequence dialog box, which displays which animation groups have images in them. You will see in Figure 7.36 that there are only two animation groups listed. Select Walking and click OK.

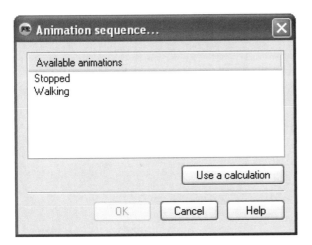

Figure 7.36
The Animation Sequence dialog box.

Now that the action has been added, press the F7 button to run the program
and wait for the button to appear before moving the mouse cursor over it.
You will notice that it goes to a lighter color. The main issue now is that
when you move the mouse away from the Play button, the highlight stays in
place.

The next event that you will create will be one that removes this highlight
when the mouse is moved off the Play object. You may have noticed when
you created the condition in event line 4 that there wasn't any option
for the mouse pointer not being over an object. This is because in TGF2, you
create your event and then change it to Negated. This means that the
opposite is true. We will now create the next event in the same way as
the previous one.

1. Click the New Condition text on event line 5. The New Condition dialog
   will appear; right-click the Mouse Pointer and Keyboard object.

2. Select the Mouse option.

3. Choose Check for Mouse Pointer over an Object. A dialog box will now
   appear, as shown in Figure 7.35. Select the Play object and click OK.

   So we now have our two events on lines 4 and 5, as shown in Figure 7.37, but
   the event line 5 needs to be the opposite of what it is currently set to.

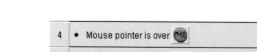

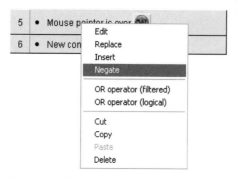

Figure 7.37
The two events: the second one needs to be the opposite of how it is currently set.

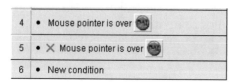

Figure 7.38
The Negate option in the pop-up menu.

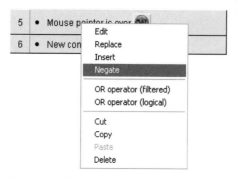

Figure 7.39
The Negate option applied to the condition in event line 5.

4. To make a condition the opposite of what it currently is, you will need to negate it. To negate the condition in event line 5, you will need to right-click the condition in event line 5.

5. A pop-up menu will appear; select the Negate option, as shown in Figure 7.38.

6. The event will now contain a big red cross next to the condition in event line 5, as shown in Figure 7.39.

So reading the event line 5, it now means: "When the mouse pointer is *not* over the Play button." Now that you have your event check when the mouse isn't over the Play button, you need to change the animation back to Stopped, which will take the Play button back to its original state.

1. Move to the right of event line 5, until you are directly under the Play object.

2. Right-click the blank action box and select Animation | Change | Animation Sequence.

3. When the Animation dialog box appears, choose the Stopped Animation text and click OK.

If you now run the frame, you will be able to move the mouse over and away from the Play button and see the switching of the animation sets.

Adding a Comment Line

Sometimes, it is useful to add a comment line either to break up the code or to describe what you are doing in a specific set of code below it. In this case, we are going to create a comment to explain what is going to happen in the code line below it.

1. Right-click the event line number 6 and select Insert | A Comment from the pop-up menu.

2. In the Edit Text box, type **Jump to next frame** and then click OK.

We are now ready to add our final event to this frame.

Playing a Sound and Moving to the Next Frame

The final event will involve checking to see when the user clicks the left mouse button on the Play object. At this stage, the actions will play a sound and move to the second frame. First, let's create the event condition that will check for the mouse click. This condition is under the Mouse Pointer and Keyboard system object.

1. Click the New Condition text on event line 7.

2. When the Condition dialog box appears, right-click the Mouse Pointer and Keyboard object and from the pop-up menu, select Mouse | User Clicks on an Object.

3. A dialog box will appear, as shown in Figure 7.40, which details different configurations that you can check when checking for a mouse click.

4. We want to keep with the defaults, so click the OK button.

Figure 7.40
The User Clicks on an Object dialog box.

5. You will now be asked for which object you want to test against. You want the Play object, so single left-click the object and click OK.

   Because we have our User Clicks with Left Button on Play Object, it's time to add your two actions. The first action is to play a sound.

6. Move to the right of event line 7, until you are under the Sound system object. Click the blank action box and select Samples | Play Sample.

7. Click the Browse button opposite the From a File option. This should take you to the Sounds folder on the CD-ROM. If not, navigate to the Game1\Sounds folder.

8. Select the Pop bubble.wav file and click Open.

   Now we need one final action to move from the current menu frame to our game frame. To do this, use the Storyboard Controls system object.

9. Still on event line 7, move across until you are under the Storyboard Controls system object.

10. Click the blank action box and select Next Frame.

    When the player clicks the Play button, it will play a short sound and then move to the next frame. It is important to remember that the process of clicking the button and moving to the next frame happens very quickly, so putting a long sound file would not work correctly because before it had finished playing, the screen would have already changed.

Congratulations! You have completed the first frame of your game. Why not press F7 and give it a go to see what happens when you click the Play button?

Programming the Game Frame

The game frame is the second screen that the player is introduced to, and it is where the player plays the game and tries to score as many points as possible. Once the player has lost his life, the game will then proceed to frame 3.

Before you start, you need to make sure you are on the correct frame:

1. Double left-click game in the Workspace Toolbar.

    You will see the game frame with the objects in place, ready for you to begin coding the logic for the game.

2. To begin coding, you will need to be in the Event Editor for the current frame, so click the Event Editor button on the toolbar.

Game Frame Components

In the game frame, you will want to achieve several things:

- Check for a collision between the bat and ball.

- Check if the ball tries to leave the top, left, or right of the screen.

- Check if the ball leaves the bottom of the screen.

- Check for a collision between the ball and a brick.

- Check to see if the player presses the Escape key.

- Check to see if all bricks have been destroyed.

- Add to the score.

- Destroy bricks.

- Go to the next frame when the ball has left the screen at the bottom.

Collision Between Ball and Bat

Our first event is quite straightforward: We want to check when the ball has hit the bat. Once it does, we want to play a sound, as this makes for a nice effect. We then need to bounce the ball, so that it goes back up toward the bricks.

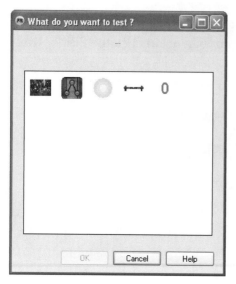

Figure 7.41
The Collision test box.

To check for a collision, the event needs you to select one of the two objects that you are going to check a collision against; it will then ask you for the second object to test against.

1. Click the New Condition text on event line 1. Select the Ball object and then Collisions | Another Object. You will then be given a dialog box, as shown in Figure 7.41, asking you to choose an object. Select the Bat object and click OK.

2. Move across from the event that you have just created until you are directly under the Sound system object. Right-click the blank action box and pick Samples | Play Sample. You will notice some sounds already listed; select Pop Bubble and click OK.

3. Move to the right of the first event line until you are directly under the ball. Right-click and select Movement | Bounce. This will enable the ball to bounce once it has hit the bat object.

   You have now created your first event for the game frame; press the F7 key to run the frame.

   On this frame, the bat has been told to use the mouse to move it to the left and right. In your own games, you would have to configure this manually, which is covered in more detail in Chapter 10. But as the mouse is controlling the bat, you will notice that you no longer have a mouse cursor to close the game. This is something you will need to change later on in this game by having a Quit key, whereby you and the players can exit the game using a specific key on the keyboard. To exit the game for now, you can hold down the ALT key and press the F4 key.

Ball Leaving the Top, Left, or Right Side of the Screen

The main aim of the game is to stop the ball from leaving the bottom of the screen and to destroy all of the bricks. If we were to run the game now, the ball would fly off in a direction and not return. We now need to program the game so that if the ball hits the top of the frame, the left, or the right, then it will bounce back into play. We won't do this for the bottom, because that is where the ball can leave, and if it does, the game will be over.

To do this we need to check the position of the ball and check if it is leaving the top, left, or right part of the screen.

1. Click the New Condition text on event line 2.

2. The New Condition dialog box will appear. Right-click the Ball object, since this is the object that you need to test. From the pop-up menu, choose Position | Test Position of Ball.

3. A Test Position of the Ball dialog box will appear. This has a number of arrows to show you the possible areas where the ball might be leaving the frame or moving into play that you might be able to test for. You want to test when the ball is leaving the top, left, and right, so click the arrows pointing outwards in these positions. We have identified these arrows in Figure 7.42. Click OK after you have selected these arrows.

4. You now need to add the action to make the ball bounce. Move across from the event on line 2 and right-click the action box directly under the Ball. Select Movement | Bounce.

Ball Leaves the Bottom of the Screen

When the ball leaves the bottom of the screen, you don't want it to bounce back into play, but it should actually go straight to the next frame. This is because as far as this game is concerned, the player only has one life. In your own games, you

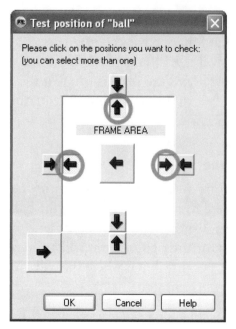

Figure 7.42
Testing the position of the ball.

may want to give the player a number of lives and remove one of them if the ball goes off the screen.

Using the same process you used to test the top, left, and right, you need to test for the ball leaving at the bottom.

1. Click the New Condition text on event line 3.

2. The New Condition dialog box will appear. Right-click the ball and choose Position | Test Position of Ball.

3. Select the down-pointing arrow so that you can test when the ball is leaving the frame; then click OK. The event will now be added.

   Now we will add the action to move to the end frame.

4. Move across until you are under the Storyboard Controls object, right-click, and select Next Frame.

   If you run the game now, the ball will bounce off the three walls and off the bat; when the ball goes off the bottom of the screen, the frame will end.

Collision Between Ball and Brick

We now need to check for a collision between the ball and the bricks. Otherwise, the game wouldn't be very interesting, since it would be just a ball bouncing around the screen. The bricks also give us the opportunity to give the player a score, and then we will display this within a high-score table. We use the same process as checking for any other collisions, but for the actions we need to play a sound, add 20 to the score, and then destroy the brick that the ball has collided with.

1. Click the New Condition text on event line 4. Select the Ball object, right-click it, and choose Collisions | Another Object. When the Test Collision dialog box appears, select the Brick object and then click OK.

   Let's now add a sound so it plays when it hits a brick.

2. Move to the right of the event on line 4, right-click the Speaker action box, and select Samples | Play Sample.

3. Click the Browse button next to From a File, and you should be in the Sounds folder. If not, navigate to the CD-ROM and then to the Game1\Sounds folder.

4. Select the HITSNTH4.wav sound file and click Open.

   Now we will add 20 to the score, which will mean that the player will get 20 points for every brick destroyed.

5. Still on event line 4, move across to the right until you are under the Player 1 object (this object resembles a joystick). Right-click the action box and select Score | Add to Score. This will allow you to add to the current score. Using the Set to Score option would reset the score to 20 every time a block was hit, which would prevent the player from getting anything over 20 points.

6. An Add to Score dialog box opens, which by default will display 0. Replace the 0 with a 20, as shown in Figure 7.43, and then click OK to save it to the Event Editor.

   Finally, you now need to destroy the brick that was hit by the ball. To do this, there is a destroy action, which is located under the object that we want to destroy, in this case, the brick.

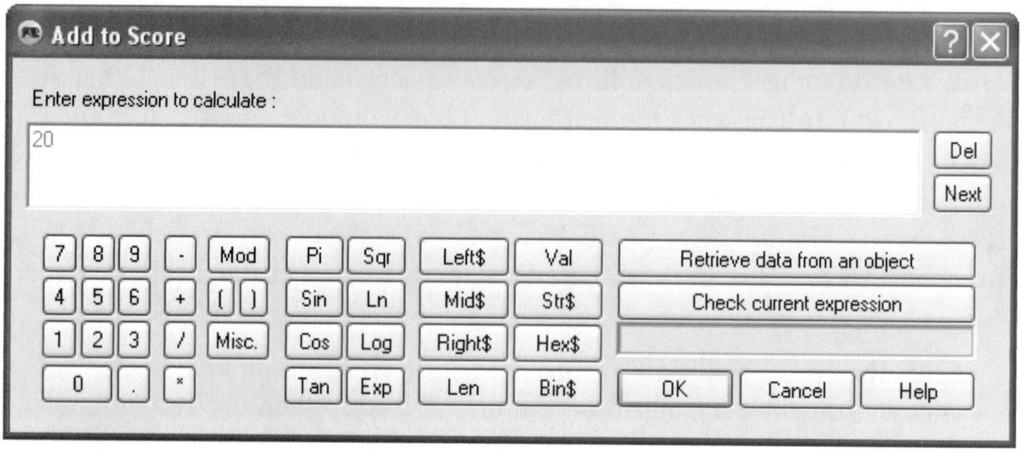

Figure 7.43
The Add to Score box.

7. Still on event line 4, move directly across until you are under the brick object, right-click the action box, and then select Destroy.

If you run the game now, you will see that it destroys the bricks once the ball hits them, plays a sound, adds 20 to the score, and when the ball goes off-screen, finishes the level.

Exiting the Game from a Key Press

As mentioned previously, except for the ball going out of play, there is no way to stop the game. It is always a good idea to allow players to exit the game when they want to. We will now add what is called an Escape key, which on old computers was a key to stop what the computer was doing. These days it doesn't do much, but is still present on the computer as Esc in the top left-hand corner. The Esc is still recognized as a way of exiting programs, mainly games, so when the user presses it, we will make the game quit. We will need to use the Mouse Pointer and Keyboard option to program it in.

1. Click the New Condition text. Select the Mouse Pointer and Keyboard object and then Keyboard | Upon Pressing a Key.

2. You will now be asked to press a key, as shown in Figure 7.44.

3. Press the Escape key (the Esc key in the top left-hand corner of the keyboard).

Figure 7.44
Upon Pressing a Key dialog box.

4. This key press will now be recorded within the Event Editor.

5. Move across from the event until you are directly under the Storyboard Controls object; right-click the action box and select End the Application.

Run the frame now, and before the ball goes out of play, press the Esc key to test that it works (which it does).

Last Brick Has Been Destroyed

In a normal game where you might have lots of different levels once the bricks have all been destroyed, you would make the game go to the next frame and start a new level. In this game, we will make the frame restart, which retains all the score information and resets everything back to its original starting position. This means the game can go on indefinitely until the player misses the ball.

1. Click the New Condition text on event line 6.

2. Select the Brick object. Then select the menu option Pick or Count | Have All Bricks Been Destroyed.

Now that the event is complete, you need to create the action, which is to restart the current frame.

3. Move across to the Storyboard Controls object and select Restart the Current Frame.

Well done! You have now completed all of the events for the game frame.

Programming the End Frame

The end frame is the third screen that the player is introduced to, and it is where the player can see if he achieved a high score or not.

Before you start, you need to make sure you are on the correct frame:

1. Double left-click on end in the Workspace Toolbar.

2. You will see the game frame with the objects in place, ready for you to begin coding the logic for the game.

3. To begin coding, you will need to be in the Event Editor for the current frame, so click the Event Editor button on the toolbar.

End Frame Components

In the end frame, you will want to achieve three things:

▪ At the start of the frame, the game should play some music.

▪ If the player presses the spacebar, it should take them to frame 1.

▪ If there is no response from the player, after 10 seconds, they should go to the first frame.

Play Some Music

Using the same process as for the first frame, let's play some music.

1. Click the New Condition text. Select the Storyboard Controls object and from the pop-up menu, pick Start of Frame.

2. Move to the right of the event until you are under the Sound object, right-click it, and select Samples | Play and Loop Sample.

3. From the Play and Loop sample dialog box, choose the Spatial Maths item from the samples listing and click OK.

4. Type in a **0** in the Repeat Count dialog box and click OK.

User Presses Spacebar

If the user wants to move back to the main frame, it is useful to provide this option either in a button or a key press. In this game, we will be using a key press of the spacebar to signal that the user wants to move back to frame 1.

1. Click the New Condition text on event line 2 and select the Mouse Pointer and Keyboard object.

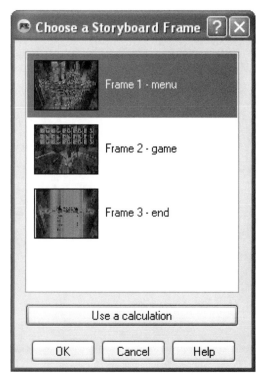

Figure 7.45
Selecting a frame to jump to.

2. Select Keyboard | Upon Pressing a Key. Then press the spacebar when the Upon Pressing a Key dialog box appears.

3. Move to the right of this event until you are under the Storyboard Controls object, right-click it, and select Jump to Frame. A dialog box will now appear, as shown in Figure 7.45, which provides a thumbnail view of the frames that you can jump back to.

4. Frame 1 is already selected, so you can click OK.

Timer Event

The last event we want to add is to move the screen from frame 3 back to frame 1 if the user hasn't pressed anything in 10 seconds. This is just an extra measure to ensure that the user goes back to the main game screen.

1. Click the New Condition text on event line 3, select the Timer object, and then select Is the Timer Equal to a Certain Value.

2. Move the slider, or type in **10,** to replace the 1 second; then click OK.

3. Move to the right of this event until you are under the Storyboard Controls object, right-click, and select Jump to Frame. A dialog box will appear, and it will already be on frame 1. Click OK.

   You have now completed all of the events for the game.

Additional Notes about the Game

There are a couple of things to note that we have touched upon in this chapter. First, you might have noticed that the ball moved on its own. This is not a normal behavior, and not all objects you create from scratch from the object list will have

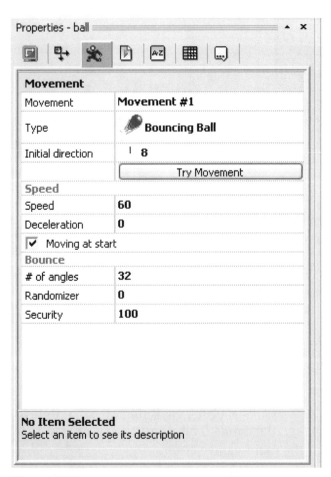

Figure 7.46
The ball already had a movement assigned to it.

any movement applied to them. Because you placed these items from a Library, they already had a set of properties applied to them. The ball had been given a ball movement, as well as its speed and directions, before you began to make the game.

You can access the movement information by going to the game frame, single left-clicking the ball to access the ball's properties, and then clicking the Movement tab. You can see an example of the properties for the ball in Figure 7.46.

You will be learning all about movement later on in the book, in Chapter 10.

The second item that you didn't configure was another type of movement, and this was for the bat to move across the screen when in the game frame. This is also accessed via the Properties dialog and the Movement tab. You can view the properties by clicking the bat and then the Movement tab. You can see that the property for the mouse is just an Edit button (see Figure 7.47). Again, you will be covering the mouse movement in Chapter 10.

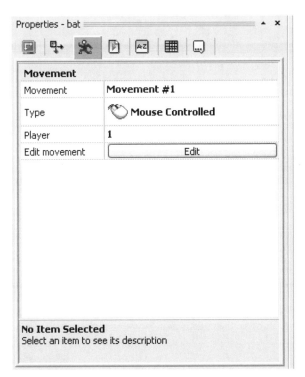

Figure 7.47
The Movement tab for the bat.

Chapter Summary

In this chapter, you have created your first game, called Future Tennis. Hopefully, this process has shown you that with very few events you can have a good working game. Once you are proficient with this program, you should be able to create a game like this in a very short time. The main thing that might take more time would be creating the artwork and finding or creating music files. However, if you use stock graphics and sounds (from the full-version CD for example), then you will be able to jump straight into making games much more quickly.

In the next chapter, we will start our second game, which is a shoot-'em-up game called Quick Draw.

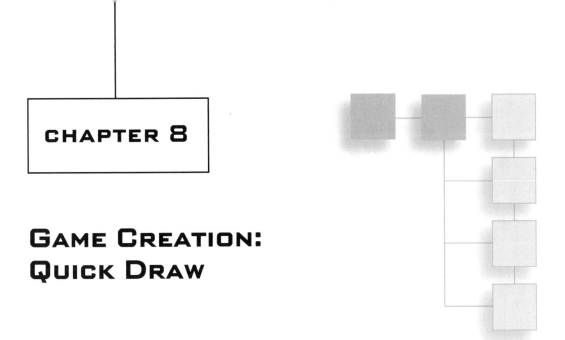

CHAPTER 8

GAME CREATION: QUICK DRAW

In this chapter:

- About the Game

- Quick Setup

- Event Programming

- Final Configuration

- Chapter Summary

In this chapter, you will make your second game, called Quick Draw. This game takes some of the concepts you have already learned about in the previous game and builds on them, but also introduces you to some features that will be new to you.

About the Game

We shall start off this chapter by giving a brief story of the game we are about to make:

> You are the new Sheriff in town, but unfortunately you may not be in the job for very long. The nasty brothers have arrived in town and have just completed a bank robbery. The stakes are high, but you are the only person who can stop them. Go into town and prevent them from escaping. Good luck.

As the story suggests, you are playing the part of a Sheriff whose job is to prevent the bad guys from escaping with their loot. The game is a simple shoot-'em-up where you control the mouse cursor and must shoot the enemy before they have a chance to shoot you. The game has a single level of difficulty, but it would be very easy for you to create additional levels if you wanted to. You can see an image of the game in progress in Figure 8.1.

The game has been split into three frames, the same as the first game you created. These frames include: the menu frame to direct the user to start the game, the game frame where the user plays the game, and finally the end frame where he will enter or see the high scores.

You should play the game before creating it, so you can get an idea of what will happen and how the game is played. You can find the game executable on the

Figure 8.1
The game Quick Draw in progress.

CD-ROM that is provided with this book, located in the Game2 folder and called Quickdraw.exe.

Quick Setup

To save you some time setting out the game and creating the frames, which you should have a good idea how to do now, we have created a file ready for you to get into the programming of the game.

You will need to copy the file Quick Draw Blank.mfa from the CD to a location on your PC's hard disk. The Quick Draw Blank.mfa file is located in the Game2 folder of the CD-ROM provided with this book. After you have copied the file, open it up and get ready to begin programming.

Event Programming

In this section of the book, we will begin to program the events that bring all the frames together to create our game. Again, we will be working on our game in the order of the frames, but in your own games you can work on them in any order you feel necessary.

Programming the Menu Frame

The menu frame is the first screen that the player is introduced to, and its main goal is to direct the player to the areas of the game that he might want to go to. From Quick Draw's menu screen, the player can only go to the game frame.

Before you start, you need to make sure you are on the correct frame by following these steps:

1. Double left-click on menu in the Workspace Toolbar.

2. You will see the menu frame with the objects in place on the frame, ready for you to begin coding.

3. To begin coding, you will need to be in the Event Editor for the current frame, so click the Event Editor button on the toolbar.

Menu Frame Components

In the menu frame, you will want to achieve three things:

- Create an event to play some music at the start of the frame.

- When the user clicks the Start button, make a sound and move to the game frame.

■ When the game is told to go to the next frame, play a zoom-in transition.

Creating the Note Event

The first thing we will do for this game is create our heading comment, which describes the name of the program, the book it is from, and the version number. In your own games, you would add as much or as little information as you like, but you might want to put a version number and a last-built date. This is a good way of tracking files and when you have made changes to them.

1. Right-click the number 1 in the Event Editor and select Insert | A Comment.

2. When the Edit Text dialog box appears, type in **Quick Draw**; then press the Return/Enter key twice, type in **An Introduction to Game Creation for Teens**, press Return twice again, and type in **Version 1.0**.

3. Click the radio button Centered.

4. Click the Choose Font button and select the style Bold and the font size of 14. Then click OK.

5. You will now be back at the Edit Text dialog. Click Set Back Color and pick a color. Once you have selected a color (preferably something light colored so you can read the text), click OK.

6. Finally, click OK to save the information to the Event Editor. You will see the event in Figure 8.2.

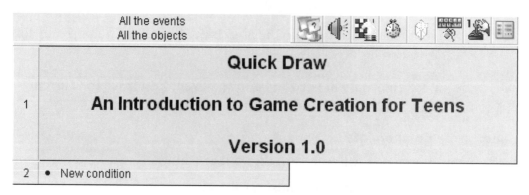

Figure 8.2
The first event is a comment line.

Start of Frame

We want to play a sound file at the start of the game, and we will do that using the Start of Frame event.

You created a couple of these conditions and actions in the first game, so hopefully you should now be a little more comfortable with the process.

1. Click the New Condition text on event line 2.

2. Select the Storyboard Controls object and select Start of Frame.

3. Move to the right of this event until you are directly under the Sound object, right-click the action box, and choose Samples | Play Sample.

4. The Play Sample dialog box will appear. Click the Browse button, opposite the From a File text. Navigate to the CD provided with this book and then into the Game2\Sounds folder.

5. Select the music.wav file and click Open. This will save the information into the Event Editor.

Player Clicks Left Mouse Button on Start_Button

So the frame will start, and it will play some music, but we need the player to be able to move between this frame and the next. To do this, we will use a simple condition that checks when the user clicks the left mouse button on an object. You may remember doing this process for the first game.

1. Click the New Condition text on event line 3. Select the Mouse Pointer and Keyboard object | The Mouse | User Clicks an Object. Leave the defaults as they are when the dialog box appears and click OK.

2. You will be asked which object the condition is going to test the mouse click against. We have only one object in use in the menu frame (this is because backdrops never appear in the list, and we only added two objects to the menu frame). Select the Start_Button object and click OK.

   We now have our condition, so it's time to add the actions. We will be adding two: the first to play a shooting sound, and the second to jump to frame 2.

3. Move to the right of the event on line 3, until you are directly under the Sound object; then right-click and select Samples | Play Sample.

4. The Sound dialog box appears. Click the Browse button for From a File, which should open up the Sounds folder for Game2. If not, then navigate to Game2\Sounds on the CD that comes with this book. Select the file Gunshot1.wav and click Open.

   Now, let's create the jump to frame 2.

5. Still on event line 3, move across to the Storyboard Controls object, right-click the action box, and select Next Frame.

Saving Progress

Save your progress as you work through this game example.

Adding a Transition

If you run the game now (the whole application by pressing F8), you will notice that the first frame will play, and the music will start. You will be able to click the Start_Button, and it will automatically take you to the game frame. You might have noticed that it didn't play the Gunshot1.wav sound on its exit of frame 1. This is because you were moving between the frames too quickly to hear the sound play. The move between frames 1 and 2 also seems a little quick and appears to jump. What you can do to fix both of these issues is to add a frame transition.

A transition is an effect that you can apply to the start or end of a frame. This will make the move from one frame to another appear smoother or allow you to create a special effect. These are very useful if you have two frames that have contrasting graphics and the move between the frames is visible to the user, often looking unprofessional or untidy. We will add a zoom transition that will zoom the screen when the user presses the Start_Button object. Because it will play at the end of the frame, it will also give the Gunshot1.wav sound time to play.

We are now going to add a transition effect to the first frame, where it will zoom inwards when the player presses the Start button.

1. To be able to add a transition you have to be in the Storyboard Editor, so click the Storyboard Editor button on the toolbar.

2. You will see the three frames of your game. Click the Fade-Out Transition Creation button, as highlighted with a circle as shown in Figure 8.3.

   The Transition Set-up dialog box will now appear, as shown in Figure 8.4. This allows you to pick from a number of built-in transitions (currently, it is

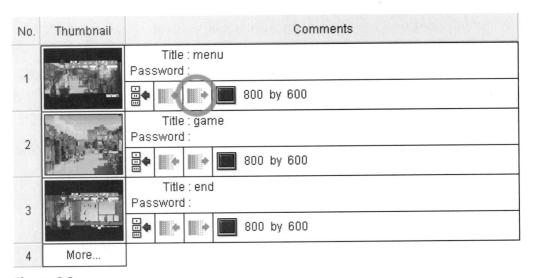

No.	Thumbnail	Comments
1		Title : menu Password :
		▦ 800 by 600
2		Title : game Password :
		▦ 800 by 600
3		Title : end Password :
		▦ 800 by 600
4	More...	

Figure 8.3
The Fade-Out Transition Creation button.

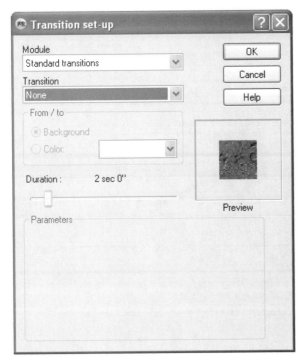

Figure 8.4
The Transition Set-up dialog box.

set to none). You can select a transition from the drop-down box, and it will show you a preview of what it will look like.

3. Click the Transition drop-down box and select Zoom 2.

4. A set of properties for this transition appears. Click Zoom In, which will make the screen zoom in toward the center of the image when it moves from frame 1 to frame 2.

We do not need to change any of the other options. Click OK to save this to the Storyboard screen. You will now notice that the Storyboard displays any transitions that are attached to the frame (see Figure 8.5).

Run the application by pressing F8 and then click the Start_Button. You can now hear the gunshot, and the screen will zoom inwards on the image, as shown in Figure 8.6. If you want try some of the other transitions to see what they look like, you can right-click the transition text in the Storyboard Editor and select Transition Setup. Remember to set it back to Zoom 2 and Zoom In before continuing. You can see the final code for the menu frame in Figure 8.7.

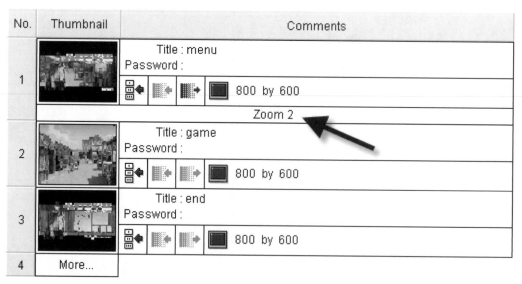

Figure 8.5
The Zoom 2 transition applied to the end of frame 1.

Figure 8.6
The Zoom 2 transition taking place in the game.

Programming the Game Frame

The game frame is the busiest screen that the player is introduced to. If you have not yet played the game fully, you should do that now so you get a good idea of what happens and can relate that back to the code.

Before you start, you need to make sure you are on the correct frame:

1. Double left-click on game in the Workspace Toolbar.

2. You will see the menu frame with the objects in place on the frame, ready for you to begin coding.

To begin coding, you will need to be in the Event Editor for the current frame, so click the Event Editor button on the toolbar.

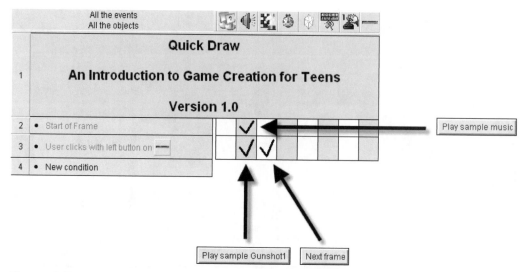

Figure 8.7
The code for the menu frame.

Game Frame Components

In the game frame you will want to achieve a number of things:

- Make some cowboys appear at various areas on the screen.

- Make the cowboys shoot guns and play a sound.

- Allow the player to shoot a gun back at the cowboys via the mouse cursor.

- Remove a life every time the player is shot.

- Add 20 to the score for every time the player defeats a cowboy.

- Go to the next frame when all lives are lost.

All three of the enemy cowboys have had a predefined path movement applied to them. Path movement allows you to draw a path on the screen to show where the cowboys should go. You can see one of the cowboys with a path assigned to it in Figure 8.8.

This is the only thing that has been set up in advance for this game frame.

Stopping Movement

We have used the Start of Frame event a few times to play a sound at the very beginning of the game. Start of Frame is also very useful when you want to set up

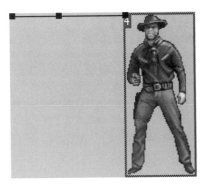

Figure 8.8
The path movement of one of the cowboys.

various options before the game has started. Our three cowboys have path movement applied to them (we discuss path movement in Chapter 10), and if they were placed on the frame, you would see them move automatically as soon as the game has started. This happens because by default the objects that have movement applied will move automatically to begin with. We need to stop them from moving, and then we can tell TGF2 to make them move again when we require them to.

Click the New Condition text and select the Storyboard Controls object and then Start of Frame.

We will now add our actions to our three cowboys, which are called Cb_1, Cb_2, and Cb_3. But before we do, you might notice that the order of the objects in the Event Editor is not to your liking, and in the case of Figure 8.9, the three cowboys are not lined up one after another, but rather another object is between Cb_1 and CB_2. What we can do is to drag and drop each object into a new order, which will help us to read the actions and keep similar objects next to each other.

1. If your cowboys are not lined up one after another, you can left-click the mouse button on a cowboy, hold it down, and drag it to a new location. In Figure 8.9, we dragged the eaten apple image after the two cowboys, and the new order is shown in Figure 8.10.

Clicking on the Action Icons

Do not single left-click on the objects displayed at the top of the Event Editor; otherwise, the program will change to display only actions for that particular object. If you accidentally do display only the actions for that particular object, you can single left-click it again to go back to the normal view.

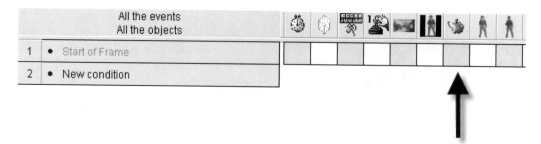

Figure 8.9
The order of our objects in the Event Editor and the object we want to move.

All the events All the objects										
1	• Start of Frame									
2	• New condition									

Figure 8.10
The new order of the objects and the location of the moved object.

Qualifier Group

You may be wondering what the half-eaten apple is doing in the object list. This is a Qualifier group, and it's a new object created by grouping other objects together. We will talk about this in more detail shortly, when we get to the events that require Qualifier groups to be used.

2. Move across to the right until you are directly under the object cb_1, right-click the action box, and select Movement | Stop.

3. You need to do the same action for the other two cowboys, and TGF2 gives you two ways of achieving this. You can manually do the same process again, or you can drag the action (checked) from cb_1 and drop it on cb_2 and cb_3.

4. Give this a try. Select the action box by single left-clicking and holding down the mouse button, drag to the empty action box in cb_2, and do the same for cb_3.

Dragging Actions into Blank Action Boxes

You are only able to drag actions for the same types of objects—for example, these three objects are all active objects.

Your actions should now look like Figure 8.11.

Picking the Three Cowboys and Starting Their Movements

Currently, our three cowboys have been placed off-screen, so they do not show up on the game frame. When the game frame is begun, randomly you want to pick a cowboy to appear at one of three specific areas on the screen, as shown in Figure 8.12. You will also set a timeframe for selecting a cowboy; the lower the time, the more quickly the cowboy will appear. This is very useful for making the game easier or harder by amending the timer.

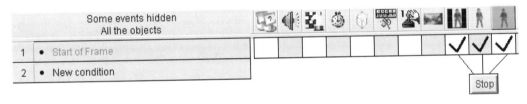

Figure 8.11
The same action for all three cowboy objects.

Figure 8.12
The current location of the cowboys and the areas where we want them to appear (shown by the numbers).

We will create a two-condition event for this. First, we need to set the timer to check every three seconds; if this is true, we need to pick at random one of the three cowboys. The easiest way to pick one of the three cowboys is to use the Pick condition. We have placed the three cowboys together since the best condition to use is one that can select the objects from a zone. A zone is a particular selected area on the frame.

1. Click the New Condition text on event line 2. Select the Timer | Every option. Change the seconds number from 1 to 3 and then click OK.

2. We have our first condition, but we want to create another in the same event, so right-click the Every 03"-00 condition and select Insert. For all conditions to do with picking and selection, you use the New Objects object. Right-click and select Pick a Random Object in a Zone. A zone selection box will appear on the Frame Editor. Draw a box around all three cowboys, as shown in Figure 8.13, and click OK.

   We need to add two actions for each cowboy: the first is to place it in the correct starting location, just off the screen, and the second is to tell the cowboy to start on its path movement. We need to do this because in the first event, we stopped the cowboys from moving. Remember that once one of the three objects in the zone has been picked, and once the selected object has been moved, it will no longer appear in that zone and will no longer be picked at random.

3. Move across from event line 2 until you are directly under cb_1; then right-click and choose Position | Select Position from the pop-up menu. When the Select Position dialog box appears, type in the x-coordinate as **70** and the y as **324**, as shown in Figure 8.14. Then click the OK button.

4. Right-click the same action box for cb_1, and select Movement | Start.

   Your actions will appear as shown in Figure 8.15.

   We now need to follow the same process on the same event line for the other two cowboys, cb_2 and cb_3.

5. Move across from event line 2 until you are directly under cb_2 and right-click and select Position | Select Position. When the Select Position dialog box appears, type in the x-coordinate to be **730** and the y to be **209**. Right-click the same action box for cb_2 and select Movement | Start.

Figure 8.13
The zone around our three enemy cowboys.

6. Move across from event line 2 until you are directly under cb_3; then right-click and select Position | Select Position. In the Select Position dialog, type in the x-coordinate to be **835** and the y to be **321**. Right-click the same action box for cb_3, and select Movement | Start.

If you now run the frame by pressing F7 or F8, you will see all three cowboys appear and then stop once they have reached their final path location, as shown in Figure 8.16.

Shooting an Enemy Cowboy

We will now create an event that will allow the player to shoot any of the three cowboys. For this we will be using a Qualifier group. As mentioned earlier, a

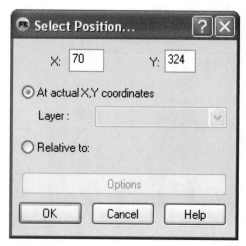

Figure 8.14
The coordinates of where we will move cb_1.

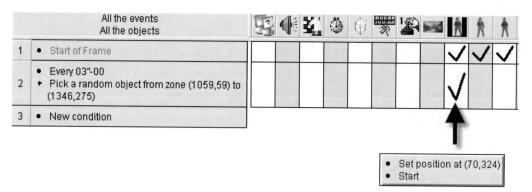

Figure 8.15
The actions for the first cowboy.

Qualifier group is a group of objects that you can put into a single group. You can then create event conditions and actions based on this group. For example, in this next event, we will be checking for when the player presses the left mouse button, but also when the user has clicked the Qualifier group containing our three cowboys.

The benefit of the Qualifier group is that if we didn't use it, we would have had to program three conditions to check to see if the user was clicking on each of the cowboys, rather than this one Qualifier, which encompasses all three. So using Qualifiers can really save you time and save the amount of code you need to write.

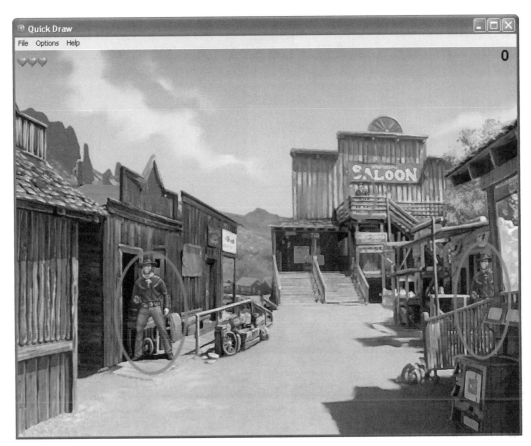

Figure 8.16
The end positions of each of the enemy cowboys.

There are a set of Qualifier groups that are premade in TGF2, some of which can be seen in Figure 8.17. These are just group names, which you can group your objects into. We will only be using one group called *Bad*.

Qualifier Groups

You create a Qualifier group by assigning it to each object individually.

Now we will create the event that will check when the user clicks the objects that are stored in the Qualifier group.

1. Click the New Condition text for event line 3.

2. Select the Mouse Pointer and Keyboard object | The mouse | User Clicks on an Object.

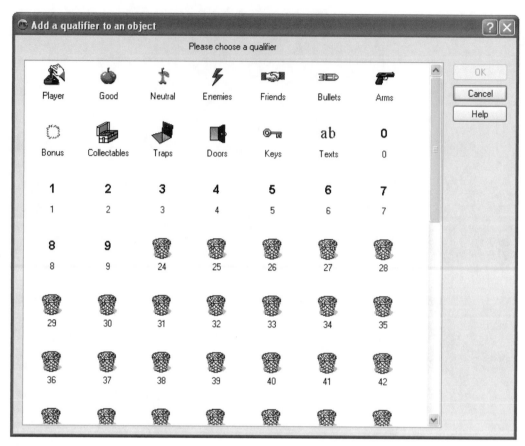

Figure 8.17
The default Qualifier groups that come with TGF2.

3. Leave the default left button, single-click the dialog box, and click OK. You will be asked which object you are going to test the left mouse click against. You want the Group.Bad object (the half-eaten apple). Click OK.

Clicking on Cowboys

> By having this event, nothing will happen unless the player's left mouse button clicks on one of the cowboys in the Qualifier group. This means that the player could left-click anywhere else on the screen, and nothing would happen.

The actions we will be making for this event are as follows:

■ Play a gunshot sound.

■ Create a bullet/shot effect.

- Add 1 to the correct cowboy Alterable Value.

- Set the gunshot to the position of the mouse.

We will now add each of these actions to complete these tasks. As you add each set of actions, run the game to see how it affects the game.

Let's first play a shooting sound:

1. Move across from event line 3 and right-click the Sound object and then select Samples | Play Sample.

2. You should see Gunshot1 in the list of samples, so single left-click it and click OK.

We will now create the Shot object. This will be the object we create and place every time the player clicks on a cowboy. First, let's create the object off-screen, and then we will move it to the mouse location.

1. Move across on the third event line until you are directly under the Create New Objects object. Right-click and select Create Object.

2. You will be given an option to select an object to create. Pick the Shot object and click OK.

3. A dialog box will appear, asking you to type in the coordinates of the object you are creating. Type in **–100** for both the x- and y-coordinates. Then click OK.

We are now going to add 1 to the cowboy's Alterable Value. Alterable Values are slots within each object that can store a variable number. A variable number is a number that can change over the course of the game. The great thing about Alterable Values is that you can write and read this data at any time. We are using Alterable Values to store a value in each of the cowboys to count how many times they have been shot by the player. If this figure reaches three, we will remove the cowboy from the screen and add some points. So, for this event, every time the object is clicked, it will add one to the total score in the Alterable Value for that object. As you are using the User Clicks with Left Button on Group.Bad, this makes things a lot easier with regard to coding. All you have to do is put the code you want to run for the clicked object in the Qualifier group. This way it will only run for the selected object, but you will only need one action rather than three.

Let's now add our action to set the Alterable Value to 1.

1. Move to the right of event line 3 until you are under Group.Bad.

2. Right-click and select Alterable Values | Add To.

3. In the Expression Evaluator, type in the number **1** and click OK.

   We now need to set the position of the Shot object we created in one of the other actions in this event and place it where the mouse is clicked. If you remember, we created a Shot object for every time the user clicks the left mouse button on the cowboys. At the moment, this object is created off-screen and is not seen. Now, we will tell it that once it has been created, it should move to the mouse cursor position. We can do this by using the Objects Position menu option and setting the mouse to the actual x- and y-coordinates.

4. Move across to the Shot object, right-click the action box, and select Position | Set X Coordinate. The Expression Evaluator will appear, asking for the x-coordinate. We want to get the current position of the mouse, so we can do this by getting the data from the mouse object into the Expression Evaluator. This will then allow us to update the position of the Shot object to the exact mouse position. You can see the Retrieve Data from an Object button in Figure 8.18.

5. Click the Retrieve Data from an Object button. You will now see a list of objects that you can bring data in from. Right-click the Mouse Pointer and

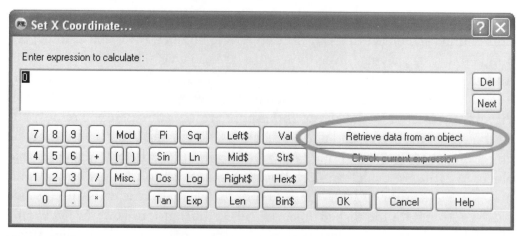

Figure 8.18
The Expression Evaluator with the Retrieve Data from an Object button highlighted.

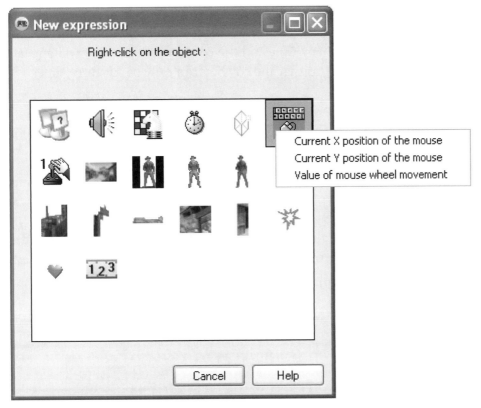

Figure 8.19
Retrieving the Current mouse position to be used to tell the Shot object where to go.

Keyboard object and select Current X Position of the Mouse, as shown in Figure 8.19.

6. This action will place the text XMouse into the Expression Evaluator; you can now click OK.

Now that we have that action reading the current x position of the mouse, we need to follow the same process but this time to read the y position.

7. Still on event line 3 and on the Shot object, right-click and select Position | Set Y Coordinate. The Expression Evaluator will appear. Click the Retrieve Data from an Object button.

8. Right-click the Mouse Pointer and Keyboard object, and select Current Y Position of the Mouse; this will write YMouse in the Expression Evaluator. Then click OK to save to the Event Editor.

If you run the game, and when the cowboys appear, you left-click on mouse, you will see the Shot object appear in the exact position where you clicked the mouse. You will notice that you can click many times on the cowboy and the shot will appear. Shortly, we will need to fix this so that the cowboy can only be hit three times.

Destroy Shot

If you try and shoot cb_2 while he is on his path movement, you will notice that it will leave a trail of shots, as shown in Figure 8.20.

We now need to destroy any shots that are no longer touching the cowboys, as this will mean that the cowboys are no longer directly over the gunshot graphics. This will ensure we don't have a trail of gunshot graphics displayed on different areas of the screen, which wouldn't look very good. We can check to see if the Shot object is overlapping any of the cowboys by using the Qualifier group Bad.

1. Click the New Condition text on event line 4.

2. Select the Shot object and then select Collisions | Overlapping Another Object.

Figure 8.20
A trail of shots left behind the cowboy's movement.

3. When the dialog box appears, select the Group.Bad object and click OK.

Currently, the event states that the Shot object is overlapping the group. We need to change it to not overlapping, and you may remember that we can do this by using the Negate option.

1. Right-click the condition in event line 4 and select Negate.

   Now, all we need to do for the action is to destroy the Shot object, since it will no longer be needed.

2. Move to the right of this event until you are under the Shot object and then right-click and select Destroy.

If you run the game now, you will notice that you can still shoot more than three times, but anything that isn't overlapping the cowboys will be removed.

Baddies Shot Three Times

We are now ready to check if the Alterable Values of any of the cowboys is equal to three, which means you have shot him three times. If the value does equal three, we will then do a number of actions. These actions are:

- Add 20 to the score.

- Remove the cowboy from the visible frame area.

- Set the path movement back to its start.

- Stop any movement, because setting it back only places it at the start, and it would just continue again. Remember the selection of the three objects.

- Set the Alterable Value back to 0 so you can start from scratch on the number of hits.

- Change the animation to Stopped. The reason for this is that the cowboy may have been playing its shooting animation, where it looks like he is shooting his gun. The cowboys only do this when they are at the end of their path movement. By resetting the animation, you ensure that it doesn't play while the cowboy is moving through its path movement when it's selected again.

- Set the position of the object. This will set it back into the zone we created earlier so that it can be randomly selected again.

First, we need to check the Alterable Value and see if it equals three. To do this, we can use the Compare option.

1. Click the New Condition text on event line 5, select the object cb_1, and then select Alterable Values | Compare to One of the Alterable Values. An Expression Evaluator will appear.

2. We stored everything in Alterable Value A, which is selected by default. It already has Equal selected, so type in the number **3**. You should now see it configured the same as in Figure 8.21.

We will now add our actions, which will all apply to event line 5.

Order of Actions

We add actions in the order that we want them to run and not necessarily in the order that the object appears in the Event Editor.

The first action we will create is to destroy the shot, as if the play is going to be removed. We don't want the shot effects left on-screen either.

1. Directly under the Shot object, right-click and select Destroy.

   Let's now add 20 to the score.

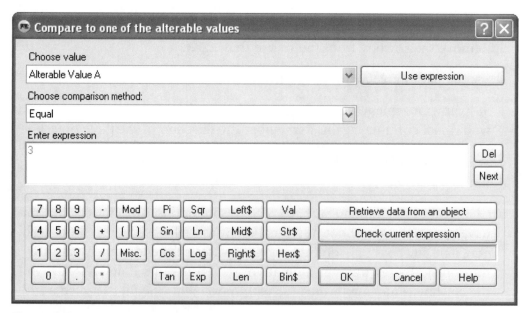

Figure 8.21
The configuration of comparing a number to an Alterable Value.

2. Directly under the Player1 object, right-click and select Score | Add to Score, type **20** in the Expression Evaluator dialog box, and click OK. All of the rest of the actions for this event are applied to cb_1. First, let's reset the path movement back to the start. Earlier, we mentioned that the reason the cowboy moves across the screen is because of the path movement that has been assigned to the object. If we don't reset this back to its original starting position, then the next time the cowboy is placed just off the frame, it will not actually move anywhere. The path movement was preconfigured, and each location on the path is called a *node*. We have a beginning and ending node, and in many cases, you can have nodes in-between. You can also rename nodes, which means you can tell an object to go back to a particular node by using its name. All three cowboys had the first node of their path movement called "start."

Path Movement

You will learn more about path movement in Chapter 10.

3. Move across until you are under the object cb_1, right-click, and select Movement | Path Movement | Branch Node. Between the quotes, type in the word **start** and then click OK.

We are now going to stop any movement so it is ready to be used again.

4. Again on the cb_1 object, right-click the action box and select Movement | Stop.

We will now set the position of the object back to outside the frame on the right-hand side. This means it will then be ready to be picked as one of the objects that can be put back into play. The reason we do this is so that the game will play as long as the player has lives left. Otherwise, no further cowboys would appear.

To set the position of the object back outside the frame, do the following:

5. Right-click the cb_1 action box and select Position | Selection Position. In the Position dialog, type **1227** for the x-coordinate and **90** for the y-coordinate. Click OK.

We need to set the Alterable Value of this object back to zero, because if we didn't and it was placed on the frame, the game would think that it had been hit three times and remove it again. This could cause the program some performance issues since this could create an endless loop, as it goes between the two events. Thus, it would keep moving the object back and forth repeatedly. To set the Alterable Value to zero, do the following:

6. Right-click cb_1 and select Alterable Values | Set. The Expression Evaluator is already set to Alterable Value A and has 0 set, so click OK.

   We now need to set the animation of the cowboy back to Stopped, which is the state that it should be in when it is just moving or waiting to get picked. The object has two animation states—the second one, which is shooting, will be programmed to make the cowboy shoot after it's reached the end of its path.

   To set the animation to Stopped, do the following:

7. Right-click the cb_1 object and select Animation | Change | Animation Sequence. The dialog box will appear. Select Stopped and click OK.

If you now run the game, you will be able to shoot cb_1 three times, and then the cowboy will disappear.

You now need to follow the same process again for cb_2 and cb_3—the only aspect that has changed is the position of the object on the frame once it's been moved. We have provided shortened instructions on how to do it so you can quickly create the next two events.

Let's now do the event and its actions for cb_2.

1. Click the New Condition text on event line 6, select the object cb_2, and then select Alterable Values | Compare to One of the Alterable Values. An Expression Evaluator will appear, so type in the number **3** and click OK.

2. Directly under the Shot object, right-click and select Destroy.

3. Directly under the Player1 object, right-click and select Score | Add to Score.

4. Type **20** in the Expression Evaluator dialog box and click OK.

5. Move across until you are under the object cb_2, right-click, and select Movement | Path Movement | Branch Node. In between the quotes, type in the word **start** and then click OK.

6. Again on the cb_2 object, right-click the action box and select Movement | Stop.

7. Right-click the cb_2 action box and select Position | Selection Position. In the Position dialog, type **1180** for the x-coordinate and **186** for the y-coordinate. Click OK.

8. Right-click cb_2 and select Alterable Values | Set. The Expression Evaluator is already set to Alterable Value A and has 0 set, so click OK.

9. Right-click the cb_2 object and select Animation | Change | Animation Sequence. The dialog box will appear. Select Stopped and click OK.

You now need to follow the same procedure once more for cb_3.

1. Click the New Condition text on event line 7, select the object cb_3, and then select Alterable Values | Compare to One of the Alterable Values.

2. An Expression Evaluator will appear, so type in the number **3** and click OK.

3. Directly under the Shot object, right-click and select Destroy.

4. Directly under the Player1 object, right-click and select Score | Add to Score.

5. Type **20** in the Expression Evaluator dialog box and click OK.

6. Move across until you are under the object cb_3, right-click, and select Movement | Path Movement | Branch Node. Between the quotes, type the word **start** and click OK.

7. Again on the cb_3 object, right-click the action box and select Movement | Stop.

8. Right-click the cb_3 action box and select Position | Selection Position. In the Position dialog, type **1097** for the x-coordinate and **92** for the y-coordinate; then click OK.

9. Right-click cb_3 and select Alterable Values | Set. The Expression Evaluator is already set to Alterable Value A and has 0 set, so click OK.

10. Right-click the cb_3 object and select Animation | Change | Animation Sequence. The dialog box will appear. Select Stopped and click OK.

You can see the events and the actions for these events in Figure 8.22.

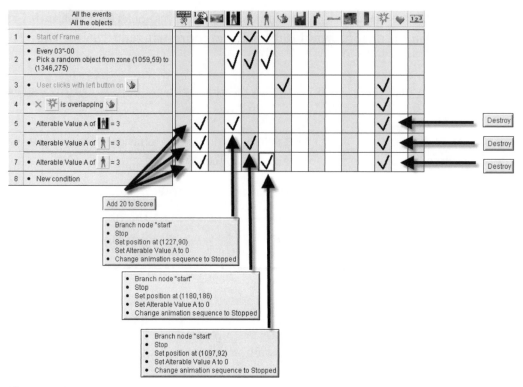

Figure 8.22
The events and actions when the cowboy has been hit three times.

Run the game now by pressing F7 or F8, and you will be able to shoot and hit each cowboy three times. They will disappear and then reappear once they have been picked randomly.

Cowboys Shooting Back

After the cowboys have reached the end of their path movement, they need to change animations to look like they are shooting back at the player. This is just a simple flashing image, which plays every few seconds.

To create the condition, we will use a condition that checks to see if an object with path movement has reached the end of its path.

We will now check to see if the cowboys have reached the end of their movement path and get them to shoot.

1. Click the New Condition text on event line 8. Select Movement | Path Movement | Has cb_1 Reached the End of Its Path.

2. Move to the right until you are under the cb_1 object, right-click, and select Animation | Change | Animation Sequence. The Animation Selection dialog box appears.

3. Choose Shooting and click OK.

Now we need to do this for cb_2.

1. Click the New Condition text on event line 9. Select Movement | Path Movement | Has cb_2 Reached the End of Its Path.

2. Move to the right until you are under the cb_2 object, right-click, and select Animation | Change | Animation Sequence. The Animation Selection dialog box appears.

3. Choose Shooting and click OK.

Now we need to do this for cb_3.

1. Click the New Condition text on event line 10. Select Movement | Path Movement | Has cb_3 Reached the End of Its Path.

2. Move to the right until you are under the cb_3 object, right-click, and select Animation | Change | Animation Sequence. The Animation Selection dialog box appears.

3. Choose Shooting and click OK.

The three events and actions look like Figure 8.23.

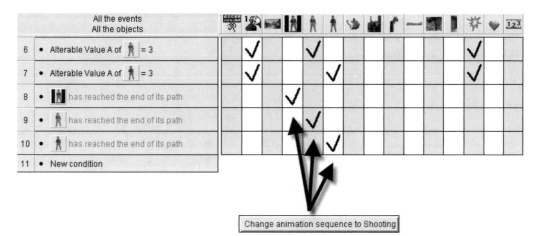

Figure 8.23
The events to make the cowboys animated to look like they are firing their guns.

Figure 8.24
The cowboys starting the shooting animation sequence.

If you run the game and wait for the three cowboys to get to the end of the path movement, you will see them changing their animation to shooting, as shown in Figure 8.24.

Subtracting Lives

We have our animations playing for the cowboys when they have finished their path movement, but now we need to subtract a life. We can do this by checking the current animation frame that is playing. When the cowboy is going through the shooting animation sequence, there is one frame where the yellow shot appears on the screen. We will check for this frame and then make a gunshot sound and subtract a life from the player.

The event also requires an Only One Action When Event Loops condition. Because the animation frames happen very quickly, it is possible for the actions to be repeated too quickly. For example, this could produce a strange noise when playing the gunshot sound. By adding the extra condition, we can ensure that it only happens once a loop.

1. Click the New Condition text on event line 11. Select the object cb_1 and then Animation | Compare Current Frame cb_1 to a Value. The Expression Evaluator will appear. We need to check if frame 1 is currently playing, so type that in the box and click OK.

2. We need to add another condition to the same event, so right-click the condition and select Insert. Select the Special object (this looks like two computer screens) and then Limit Conditions | Only One Action When Event Loops.

   You will have your conditions, so let's add the actions to play a sound and subtract a life.

3. Move across to the Sound object, right-click, and select Samples | Play Sample. Click the Browse button opposite the From a File text; a dialog box appears, and it should already be in the Sounds folder for Game2. If not, then navigate to the CD-ROM drive that contains the CD from this book and then into the Game2\Sounds folder. Select the Gunshot2.wav file and click Open.

4. Move across to the Player1 object, right-click, and select Number of Lives | Subtract from Number of Lives.

5. The Expression Evaluator appears. Type in the number **1** and click OK.

Let's follow the same procedure for cb_2 so that if he shoots, the player loses a life.

1. Click the New Condition text on event line 12. Select the object cb_2 and then select Animation | Compare Current Frame cb_2 to a Value.

2. Type in **1** in the Expression Evaluator and click OK.

3. Right-click the condition and select Insert. Select the Special object and then select Limit Conditions | Only One Action When Event Loops.

4. Move across to the Sound object, right-click, and select Samples | Play Sample. You will see the sample Gunshot2 in the Samples list. Click it and then OK.

5. Move across to the Player1 object, right-click, and select Number of Lives | Subtract from Number of Lives.

6. The Expression Evaluator appears. Type in the number **1** and click OK.

Once more we have to do it, this time for cb_3.

1. Click the New Condition text on event line 13. Select the object cb_3 and then select Animation | Compare Current Frame cb_3 to a Value.

2. Type in **1** in the Expression Evaluator and click OK.

3. Right-click the condition and select Insert. Select the Special object and then Limit Conditions | Only One Action When Event Loops.

4. Move across to the Sound object, right-click, and select Samples | Play Sample. You will see the sample Gunshot2 in the Samples list. Click it and then OK.

5. Move across to the Player1 object, right-click, and select Number of Lives | Subtract from Number of Lives.

6. The Expression Evaluator appears. Type in the number **1** and click OK. You can see the events in Figure 8.25.

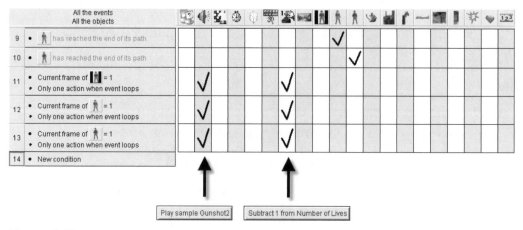

Figure 8.25
The events for the three cowboys.

If you run the game now and don't shoot at the cowboys, you will notice that they will shoot at you, and you will lose your lives.

No More Lives

We have one final event to create, and that is to check how many lives the player has left. If this number equals 0, then the player need to go to the high-scores end screen. Let's check the player's lives when it reaches zero:

1. Click New Condition in event line 14.

2. Select the Player1 object (that looks like a joystick) and then choose When Number of Lives Reaches 0.

3. Move across to the Storyboard Controls object, right-click, and select Next Frame.

Programming the End Frame

The end frame is where the player will see the high-scores table.

Before you start, you need to make sure you are on the correct frame:

1. Double left-click end in the Workspace Toolbar.

2. You will see the menu frame with the objects in place on the frame, ready for you to begin coding.

3. To begin coding, you will need to be in the Event Editor for the current frame, so click the Event Editor button on the toolbar.

Game Frame Components

We only require two events for the final frame; these will do the following:

- At the start of the game, play some music.

- After 5 seconds, go back to frame 1.

Start of Frame

At the start of the frame, we want to play the music file.

1. Click New Condition on event line 1.

2. Select the Storyboard Controls object and then select Start of Frame.

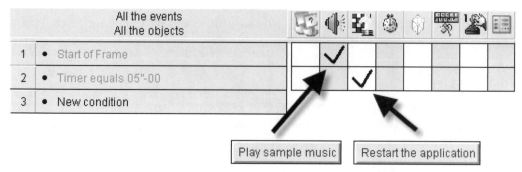

Figure 8.26
The final two events for this game.

> 3. Move across to the Sounds object and then Samples | Play Sample. You will notice the file called *music* listed in the Samples list; select it and click OK.

After Five Seconds

Just to make sure that the game goes back to the menu frame without any user interaction, after five seconds, the program will automatically take the game back. To accomplish this task, do the following:

1. Click the New Condition text and select the Timer object.

2. Select Is the Timer Equal to a Certain Value. The dialog box appears.

3. Change the 1 second to 5 seconds and click OK. Move across to the right until you are under the Storyboard Controls object and then select Restart the Application.

You can see both events and actions in Figure 8.26.

Final Configuration

The game is now complete, but there are two things we can change to make the game react better to the user. If you look at the top right-hand corner of the game window, you will notice that there are three buttons, as shown in Figure 8.27. The first allows the user to minimize the window, the second allows the user to maximize, and the third is to close the window.

The game has not been configured to disable Maximize, because this feature allows the user to make the game take up the whole of the Windows screen. In some games this is a nice feature, but in others it looks untidy, and it can be a

Figure 8.27
The Minimize, Maximize, and Close buttons.

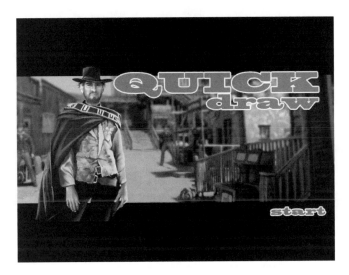

Figure 8.28
The Maximize feature switched on.

good idea to disable maximizing to prevent this. You may want to try different combinations for different types of games to see if you like them or not.

Figure 8.28 shows our Quick Draw game maximized.

Another feature that is similar to Maximize is the Thick Frame option. This feature allows the user to hold down the mouse button on the window frame and drag it to make it bigger. The problem with this is that it can allow the user to make the

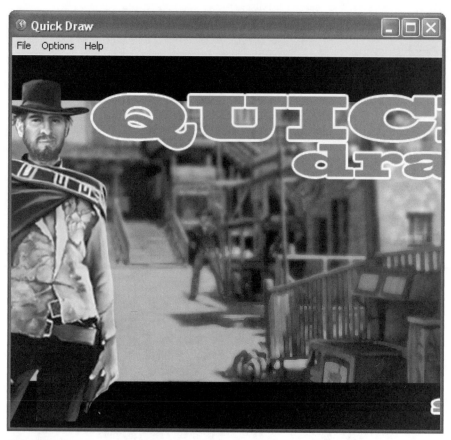

Figure 8.29
The Thick Border option in use on the Quick Draw game.

screen size totally different than what the game requires. You can see an example of the Thick Frame in use in Figure 8.29.

Both these options can be turned off very quickly with the following steps:

1. Click the Quick Draw text in the Workspace Toolbar to access the Application Properties.

2. Click the Window tab in the Properties Toolbar, which can be seen in Figure 8.30.

3. To change these two settings, check the No Maximize Box and No Thick Frame options.

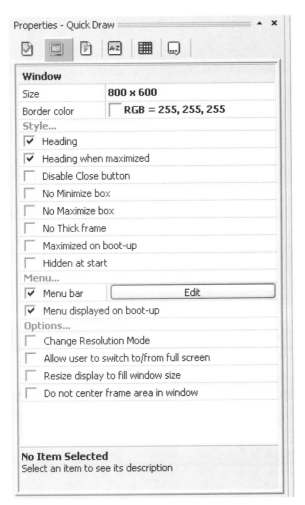

Figure 8.30
The Maximize and No Thick Frame settings.

Chapter Summary

In this chapter, you have created the cowboy shoot-'em-up game Quick Draw. You will have cemented some skills and learned some new ones while creating this exciting game. You should now begin to feel comfortable in TGF2 and using its editors. If there is something you are not sure about, go back and read it again. Don't worry too much if you are still not too sure about certain areas, because with a little more practice it will become second nature. In the next chapter, we will make our third and final game, which involves a car race.

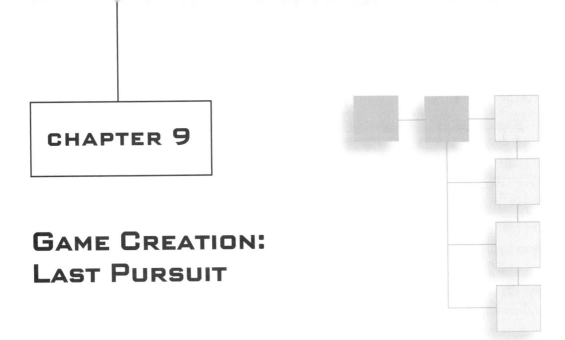

CHAPTER 9

GAME CREATION: LAST PURSUIT

In this chapter:

- About the Game

- Quick Setup

- Event Programming

- Improving the Game

- Chapter Summary

In this chapter, we will take a look at our third game, called *Last Pursuit*. Last Pursuit is a scrolling game where you are racing through a city street, dodging any vehicles that get in the way. This game will show a new feature, screen scrolling, where you will be able to scroll an image over the screen and make it look like your vehicle is actually moving.

About the Game

We shall start off this chapter by giving a brief story of the game we are about to make:

> *You are an undercover cop who is in pursuit of a major criminal. Your job is to race as fast as you can through the city streets. Unfortunately, criminals have crashed a number of vehicles along the way. Try to get through the city without hitting any vehicles, and perhaps this won't be your last pursuit.*

As the story suggests, you are playing the part of a police car driver. You are not actually chasing any vehicles in this game, but you are effectively playing dodgeball. Your goal is to navigate through the city without crashing into any trucks.

Though the game is very simple, it has a lot of scope for you to add more features to it. We are covering this game because the scrolling techniques you will use can be very important for any scrolling game that you intend to make. You can see an example of a game in progress in Figure 9.1.

You should actually play the game before creating it, so you can get an idea of what will happen and how the game is played. You can find the game executable on the CD-ROM that is provided with this book, located in the Game3 folder and called Lastpursuit.exe.

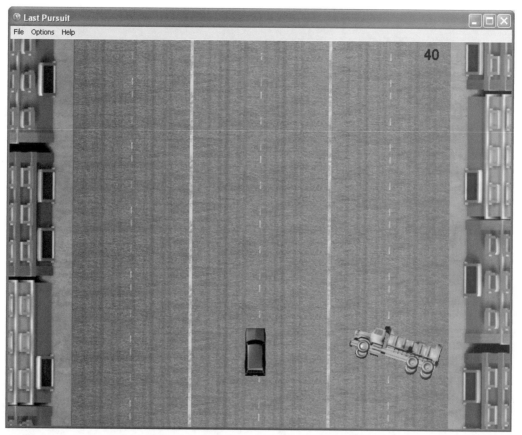

Figure 9.1
Last Pursuit in progress.

Quick Setup

To save you some time setting out the game and creating the frames, which you should have a good idea how to do now, we have created a file ready for you to get into the programming of the game. All three frames have already been created, and an eight-direction movement has been applied to the racing car.

You will need to copy the file Last Pursuit Blank.mfa from the CD-ROM onto a location on your PC's hard disk. The Last Pursuit Blank.mfa file is located in the Game3 folder of the CD-ROM provided with this book. Once you have copied the file, open it up, ready to begin programming.

Event Programming

Now, let's begin to program the events that will bring all the frames together to create our game.

Again, we will be working on our game in the order of the frames, but in your own games you can work on them in any order you feel necessary.

Programming the Menu Frame

Let's now start programming the menu frame.

Before you start, you need to make sure you are on the correct frame:

1. Double left-click on menu in the Workspace Toolbar.

2. You will see the menu frame with the objects in place on the frame, ready for you to begin coding.

3. To begin coding, you will need to be in the Event Editor for the current frame, so click the Event Editor button on the toolbar.

Menu Frame Components

In the menu frame, you will want to achieve a few things:

- At the start of the frame, play some music.

- When you move the mouse over the Start_Button, make a graphic effect appear, which will highlight the graphic.

- When you move the mouse away from the Start_Button, make the graphic effect disappear, which will highlight the graphic.

- When the user clicks on the Start_Button, move to the game frame.

Creating the Note Event

Let's create our note for the game.

1. Right-click the number 1 in the Event Editor and select Insert | A Comment.

2. When the Edit Text dialog box appears, type in **Last Pursuit**, press the Return key twice, type in **An Introduction to Game Creation for Teens**, press Return twice again, and type in **Version 1.0**.

3. Click the radio button Centered.

4. Click the Choose Font button and select the style Bold and the font size of 14; then click OK.

5. You will now be back at the Edit Text dialog. Click Set Back Color and pick a color. Once you have selected a color (preferably something light-colored so you can read the text), click OK.

6. Finally, click OK to save the information to the Event Editor.

7. You will see the event in Figure 9.2.

Start of Frame Playing a Song

We want to play a tune at the very start of the frame. The sound file we will use is very short, so you will need to use the loop option.

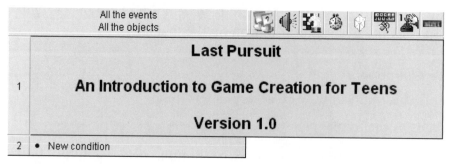

Figure 9.2
The first event is a comment line.

1. Click the New Condition text.

2. Select the Storyboard object and then click Start of Frame.

3. Move across to the right until you are directly under the Sound object, right-click, and pick Samples | Play and Loop Samples. The Play dialog box will appear.

4. Click the Browse button opposite From a File. Navigate to the CD-ROM until you are in the Game3\Sounds folder. Select music.wav and click Open. Type **0** in the Expression Evaluator and click OK.

Mouse Pointer over the Start Button

We need to create an event that shows the graphic being highlighted when the user moves the mouse over the Start_Button. This will create an animated button effect.

1. Click the New Condition text on event line 3. Select the Mouse Pointer and Keyboard object and then The Mouse | Check for Mouse Pointer over an Object. When the dialog box appears, select the Start_Button and click OK.

2. Move across to the Start_Button action box and select Visibility | Make Object Reappear.

Mouse Pointer Is Not over the Start Button

We now need to make the Start_Button go back to its original unhighlighted state if the mouse is not over it, which we can do by using the Negate option.

1. Click the New Condition text on event line 4. Select the Mouse Pointer and Keyboard object; then select The Mouse | Check for Mouse Pointer over an Object. When the dialog box appears, select the Start_Button and click OK.

2. Right-click the condition that you have just added and select Negate. A red cross will now appear at the start of the condition.

3. Move across to the Start_Button action box; then select Visibility | Make Object Invisible.

User Clicks Move to Next Frame

We now want to move to the game frame when the user clicks the Start_Button.

1. Click the New Condition text on event line 5. Select the Mouse Pointer and Keyboard object; then select The Mouse | User Clicks an Object. When the dialog box appears, stick with the defaults and click OK.

2. Select the Start_Button object and click OK.

3. Move across to the Storyboard Controls object and select Next Frame.

If you now run the frame, you'll be able to hear the game's music playing and you'll be able to highlight the Start_Button and click it, which will take you to the next frame.

Programming the Game Frame

We are now going to program the game frame. Most of the code in the game frame should be straightforward for you to follow. The new concept, which we haven't discussed before, is scrolling.

We are going to use a technique to scroll the screen that involves the following conditions:

■ Setting the screen/frame to center on the car object. This allows the car to always appear in the same position, rather than moving up or down in the frame.

■ The car will be able to move left or right.

■ The background will physically move and will continue to reappear to make it look like the road is moving.

■ You can scroll vertically or horizontally in TGF2. (We will be doing it vertically because the car will be moving upwards.)

■ You will need to set a number to one of the settings to tell it to scroll.

■ A number is set at all times to tell TGF2 the location of the object that is scrolling.

■ When an object looks like it is scrolling upwards, it starts from a high number position and works downwards. Once this position number reaches 0, then the scrolling will stop. When you want to check the y-coordinate, remember that it will be continuously reducing. When an object looks like it is scrolling downwards, it starts from a low number (1) and will always continue to scroll. But the y-coordinate will always increase.

Hopefully as we create the code for this second frame, you will understand this concept better.

Setting the Virtual Height

In any game you make, you can set a virtual height and width. This is different from a frame application size, as the frame size is an actual screen size that the user sees. When you have a scrolling game, you might want to scroll the world, and to do this you are actually moving the frame play area still within this window. By setting this number to −1, we are effectively telling TGF2 that the screen will scroll nearly indefinitely.

To set the virtual height for the game frame:

1. Click the text game in the Workspace Toolbar to bring up the game frame properties. Ensure that the Settings tab is selected and then type −1 into the Virtual Height box, as shown in Figure 9.3.

If you run the game frame now, you will see the car at the bottom of the screen, and you will be able to move it left and right. This is because the car has an eight-direction movement applied, although we have disabled all but the left and right keys, as we will move the car automatically without the need for the user to press anything.

Setting Up the Layer

In your TGF2 games, you can have many layers. Layers allow you to have graphics overlapping one another, which allows you to create special effects like in a space scene. This space scene could have stars moving in one direction and planets moving at a different speed to create amazing effects. In the game Last Pursuit, we need to tell the game that it should wrap all background images vertically. The background images in this game are the left and right images of houses and the middle road image. If you have other backdrop images, you would have to put them onto a different layer.

We need to ensure that the Layers Toolbar is switched on and visible. The Layers Toolbar is a property box that is displayed on the right-hand side of TGF2. If this toolbar is not available, do the following to switch it on:

1. Choose View | Toolbars | Layers Toolbar. This will make the Layers Toolbar appear. Left single-click the small thumbnail image of the layer. This will open up the Layers properties in the Properties Toolbar.

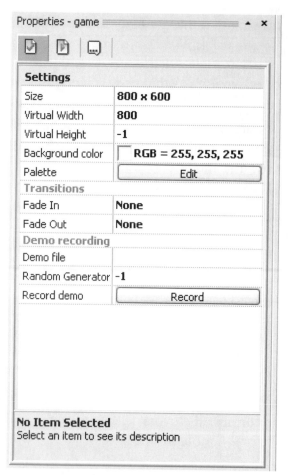

Figure 9.3
Setting up the frame scrolling.

2. Ensure that you uncheck Save Background, as this would paint the image onto the frame. You wouldn't notice that in this game, but painting the image to the frame will take up memory, albeit a small amount.

3. Click Wrap Vertically to make the images automatically appear in a continuous repeating format. You can see this Properties box in Figure 9.4.

You have set up all the properties for the game, so now it's time to complete the programming.

Click the Event Editor button to access the events sheet for the game frame.

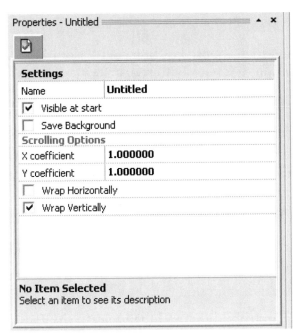

Figure 9.4
The Layers properties.

Start of Frame

We need two actions to happen at the start of our frame: First we need to play and loop some music, and then we need to set the position of the car on the virtual frame. Remember, we said the virtual frame is our scrolling area. We need to set this to a high number because the number will decrease over time, so in this case, set it to 10,000,000. This is just a high number we have selected, and this number will allow around nine hours of scrolling, so definitely enough for the player playing this game.

We will now create our virtual frame at the start of the game and play some music:

1. Click the New Condition text on event line 1. Select Storyboard Controls and then Start of Frame.

2. Move across to the Sound object and select Samples | Play and Loop Sample. When the dialog box appears, select the music file that is already in the Samples list and click OK.

3. Type the number **0** in the Expression Evaluator and click OK.

4. Move across to the Car object and then choose Position | Set Y Coordinate. When the Expression Evaluator appears, type in 10,000,000 and click OK.

Center Display on Car

By telling the frame to center on the car, that means when the car moves, it always stays in the same central position. We don't want the car to be dead center, as there needs to be some room for the player to make a split-second decision to move out of the way of any trucks.

We will now center the car at the bottom of the screen:

1. Click the New Condition text on event line 2. Select the Specials object and then Always. (Be sure to use the Always command so that this always happens.)

2. Move across to the Storyboard Controls object and then select Scrollings | Center Window Position in Frame.

3. Click the Relative To radio button and then type in **0** in the x-coordinate and then –150 in the y-coordinate box, as shown in Figure 9.5.

4. Click OK to save to the Event Editor.

This means that you will position the center of the window to the location of the car. If you wanted it truly in the middle of the screen, you would have entered 0

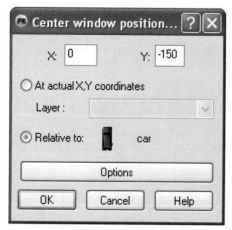

Figure 9.5
Setting the screen to a position.

and 0 for the coordinates. In this case, we are happy for the x position to be in the center of the screen (from left to right), but for the top-to-bottom position, we need the car a little farther back, so we entered −150.

Adding a Truck

We are now, every 2.06 seconds, going to add a truck to get in the way of the driver. You will need to use the Create option to create a new truck every 2.06 seconds. As we are using the virtual width, we can't use normal positioning coordinates (remember, it started at 10,000,000). This can be made easier by getting the current y position of the car and then taking 550 from that figure to place it off at the top of the screen. So shortly afterwards, it will appear on top of the frame. This is because when the screen is moving upwards, the y position number is reducing, so by taking 550 off of it, the truck will appear very soon after it's created. We will then want to position it randomly on the screen on the x-coordinate (left to right). Use the random number feature to place it at a random location on the screen (this will be explained shortly). Finally, we will need to take into account the houses on the left- and right-hand sides of the screen where we don't want the truck to overlap.

Let's start by adding the timer to check each time that 2.06 seconds has been reached:

1. Click the New Condition text on event line 3.

2. Select the Timer object and pick Every. The Timer dialog box will appear.

3. Type in 2 for the seconds and 06 in the 1/100 box. Click OK.

We will now create truck1 at a position off-screen, so we can position in another action correctly.

1. Move across to the right until you are under the Create Object object; then select Create Object. Pick truck1 from the Create Object dialog box.

2. The Location dialog will appear. We will use actual coordinates, so type in **393** for the x- and **301** for the y-coordinate. Then click OK.

If your scrolling area was smaller, it would be better to place objects at the side of the frame so they would be out of the way. Otherwise, there is a chance that they could appear on-screen, when you don't require them. In the case of Last Pursuit, the scroll area will scroll for about nine hours, so this is not something you have to worry about in this game.

Now, let's set the y-coordinate of the truck that we just created to the y position of the car, but then add a −550 to the calculation to put the truck just off the top of the screen. This means that rather than waiting nine hours for a truck to appear, it will appear almost immediately.

1. Still on event line 3, right-click the action box for truck1, as this is the object you want to move. On the action box, choose Position | Set Y Coordinate. The Expression Evaluator appears.

2. Click the Retrieve Data from an Object button, as you want to get the current car coordinates.

3. Select the car object and from the pop-up menu, choose Position Y Coordinate.

   This will place y ("car") into the Expression Evaluator. So if the game were to be scrolling at the moment, it would create a truck at the car's location, which wouldn't work because suddenly the truck would appear and then fly off the screen. So type in –550 after the command in order to create the following command in Figure 9.6.

4. Click OK to save this information to the Event Editor.

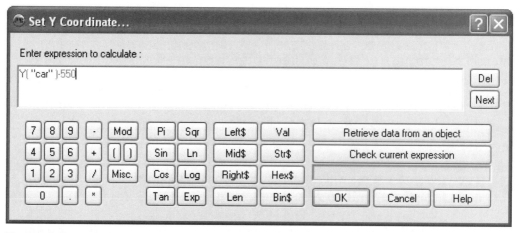

Figure 9.6
The Expression Evaluator command.

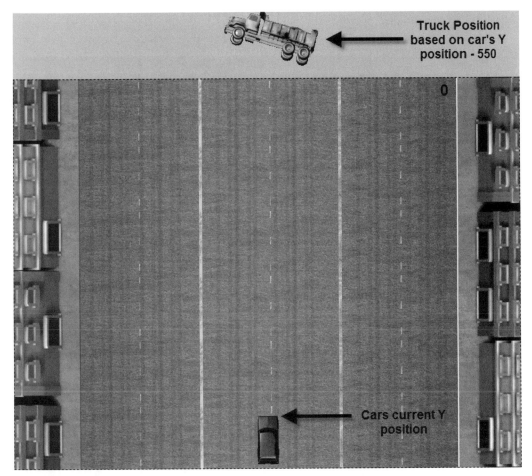

Figure 9.7
The x-coordinate positioning of the truck.

You can see why we did this in Figure 9.7.

Now that we have sorted the y position of the truck, we need to think about the position it will appear on the x-coordinate, which is the left- or right-hand side of the screen. We don't want it to appear on the left- or right-hand side of the screen where the buildings are. See Figure 9.8 for an example of places where the truck could be placed at the moment.

You will notice in Figure 9.8 that the width of the left-hand side of the screen is 100. We do not want a truck to appear here. You will notice that the area where we do want the truck to appear is 600 long, and finally the last bit of screen is again 100, and we do not want the truck to appear there.

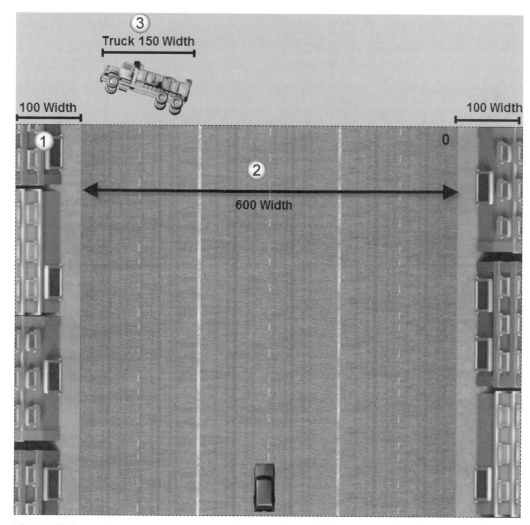

Figure 9.8
The screen sizes of objects we are dealing with.

To place the truck at differing locations, we can use the Random(N) command. The Random command tells TGF2 to pick a random number, which in this case is going to be used for the position of the truck on the x-coordinate (left to right). The command goes into the Expression Evaluator in the format of:

```
Random(N)
```

N is the range of random numbers we want to test. So, for example, you could type in:

```
Random(4)
```

This would create a random number between 0 and 3 (the 4 equates to the total number of random numbers including 0). So if we did Random (10), we would be creating random numbers between 0 and 9.

It is slightly harder in this case, as you want to place an object at a random location, which also must take into account that you don't want it in the first 100 or the last 100 of the screen coordinates. Think about the following Random command:

```
Random(5) + 1
```

If you were doing a random number to simulate a six-sided die, you wouldn't be able to use Random(6), since there is no 0 on a die, and you wouldn't be able to use Random(7) as this would use 0–7. So a good way to fix this is to add a number to the Random group, which means that if we add one we will never get the number 0. When doing this, you must always remember to reduce the total number in the brackets. For example, if you were to do:

```
Random(6) + 1
```

then you would always get between 1 and 7 as an answer. So in this case, we don't want the truck to appear in the first 100, so we can use Random(N) + 100 so as not to appear on the left-hand side. We have another problem, and that is the number that we would use where "N" is represented. You could say that the number we require is 600, as 600 + 100 is 700, which means that the truck could be positioned anywhere from 100 to 700 on the x-coordinate, which according to the screen is the total distance we are looking at. But if the truck is placed on the maximum x-coordinate position, look at Figure 9.9 to see what happens.

You will notice that we didn't take the truck's size into consideration, so when placed at the maximum position, it overlaps on the right-hand side. Now, taking this into account, let's work out the length that we can use.

- Must start at 100.

- Actual length of second part is 600.

- Truck's width is 150.

So we can calculate that 600 − 150 = 450.

So our random number would be

```
Random(450) + 100
```

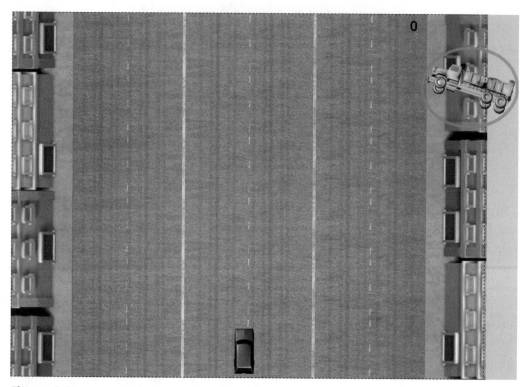

Figure 9.9
The location of the truck on the screen.

This will ensure that the values will always be above 100, and will never go above 550, which when taking into account the size of the truck will mean that its full length will never be longer than 700. And 700 is the total length of the area that we can work on. Now we need to add the action.

1. On the truck action box for event line 3, right-click and select Position | Set X Coordinate. The Expression Evaluator appears; type in:

   Random(450) + 100

   as shown in Figure 9.10 and then click OK.

Creating a Second Truck

We will now create a second truck on the screen to make the game harder. This time we will place one every 3.5 seconds. These are just random times that were selected once the game was running and the game was tested. When making your own game, you may need to enter different numbers and then change them to make the game more playable.

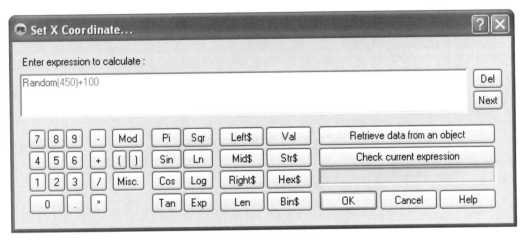

Figure 9.10
The Random command in use for our game.

To add a second truck:

1. Click the New Condition text on event line 4. Select the Timer object and then Every.

2. In the Timer dialog, type **3** for seconds and **50** in the 1/100 box, which will make 3.5 seconds. Click OK.

3. Move across to the right until you are under Create Object and select it. Pick truck2 from the Create Object dialog box.

4. The location dialog will appear. We will use actual coordinates, so type in **136** for the x- and -41 for the y-coordinate. Then click OK.

5. Still on event line 3, right-click the action box for truck2, because this is the object you want to move. Right-click the action box and choose Position | Set Y Coordinate.

6. The Expression Evaluator appears. Click the Retrieve Data from an Object button, since you want to get the current car coordinates.

7. Select the car object and then from the pop-up menu, choose Position Y Coordinate. This will place y("car") in the Expression Evaluator. We want to place it farther back on the screen. This is useful because if at any time the timers on event lines 3 and 4 ever meet, then both trucks would appear at

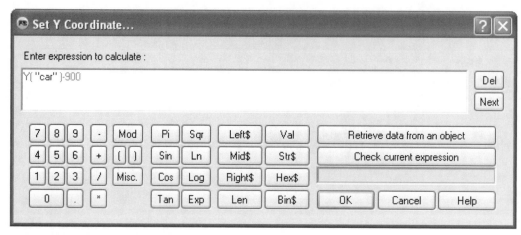

Figure 9.11
The y position with a minus figure added.

the same y location. So at the end of the expression, type in **–900.** It should now read as Figure 9.11.

8. On the truck2 action box for event line 4, right-click and select Position | Set X Coordinate. The Expression Evaluator appears; type in:

    Random(450) + 100

9. Then click OK.

Moving the Screen

We have created our trucks at intervals, but now we need to move the screen. There were two ways we could do this: We could move the screen based on the user pressing the keyboard, or, as in this case, we could move the screen automatically. The benefit of doing the second option is that the user has the choice to stop the car and move out of the way of the trucks. In addition, with the screen moving automatically, the user can only move left or right, so this provides a more difficult challenge.

We will scroll by setting a condition of Always, and then moving the position of the car based on its current position, minus a y-coordinate value. Remember that when scrolling upwards, the y-coordinates start high and count downwards, so we will need to subtract a y-coordinate off the current car's y position. I have already tested this and will use the number 15. If you want to slow the speed of the car, you would reduce this number even further, or you could speed it up by increasing the number.

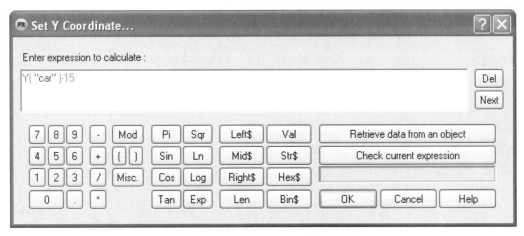

Figure 9.12
The y-coordinate of the car, minus 15 to move the screen upwards.

We will now change the car's Y position so that it appears to be moving:

1. Click the New Condition text on event line 5. Select the Special object and then Always.

2. Move across until you are directly under the car. Then right-click the action box and pick Position | Set Y Coordinate. Click the Retrieve Data from an Object button and select the Car object, Position | Y Coordinate.

3. You will now have Y("car") in the Expression Evaluator. Type in **–15** at the end, as shown in Figure 9.12.

If you run the game now, you will see the car is moving upwards, and the trucks are appearing at random places on the screen.

Adding to the Score

We need to create a way for the player to get a score, and in this case, we can just use the amount of time they drive for as the scoring system. The longer the player survives, the bigger score he gets.

We will create an event that adds 20 to the score for every one second of time that has passed, using the following steps:

1. Click the New Condition text on event line 6. Select the Timer object and then Every. When the Timer dialog appears, leave it at 1 second and click OK.

2. Move across until you are under the Player 1 object; then select Score | Add to Score. In the Expression Evaluator, type in **20** and click OK.

If you run the game now, you will see the car moving and the score adding up every second.

Stopping the Car from Moving Off-Screen

In Figure 9.12 (and if you have run the game), you may notice that the car can move off the left- and right-hand sides of the screen. You can prevent this by checking the x-coordinates of the car and testing to see if they're below 100 or above 640.

Restricting the Car's Movement

You might be wondering why we're using 640. This is again taking into consideration the width of the car. If the figure were 700 to take into account the 600+100 of the first two backdrop objects, then the car would appear on the sidewalk.

1. Click the New Condition text on event line 7. Click the car object and choose Position | Compare X Position to a Value.

2. The Expression Evaluator will appear. Change the drop-down box to read Lower and then type in **100,** as shown in Figure 9.13. Click OK.

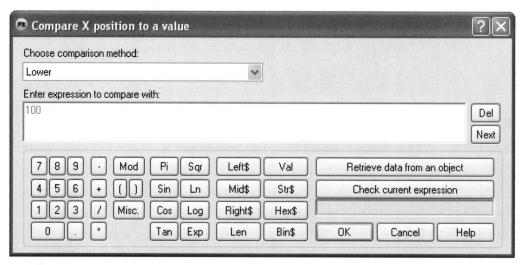

Figure 9.13
Testing the car's x-coordinate position.

3. Move across until you are directly under the Car object and then select Position | Set X Coordinate. In the Expression Evaluator, type in **100** and click OK.

This means that whenever the car tries to go below 100, the car will always be placed back at its original location of 100. Now we need to do this for the right-hand side of the screen.

4. Click the New Condition text on event line 8. Click the Car object and choose Position | Compare X Position to a Value. The Expression Evaluator will appear.

5. Change the drop-down box to read Greater and then type in **640**. Click OK.

6. Move across until you are directly under the Car object and choose Position | Set X Coordinate. In the Expression Evaluator, type in **640** and then click OK.

The car will no longer be able to leave the screen.

Collision Between Car and Trucks

The final two events for this frame involve checking when there is a collision between the car and either of the two trucks. When this happens, we will move to the highscore frame. To create the actions for the collision and its relevant actions, do the following:

1. Click New Condition for event line 9 and select the Car object; then choose Collisions | Another Object.

2. Select Truck1. Move across to the Storyboard Controls option and then pick Next Frame.

3. Click New Condition for event line 10, select the Car object, and then choose Collisions | Another Object and select Truck2.

4. Then move across to the Storyboard Controls option and pick Next Frame.

You have now finished the programming for the game frame, for which you can see the events in Figure 9.14.

Run the frame and test what you have done.

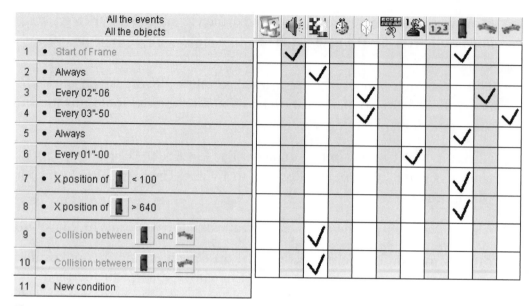

Figure 9.14
The final conditions for the game frame.

Programming the Highscore Frame

Let's now start programming the highscore frame.

Before you start, you need to make sure you are on the correct frame:

1. Double left-click highscore in the Workspace Toolbar.

2. You will see the menu frame with the objects in place on the frame, ready for you to begin coding.

3. To begin coding, you will need to be in the Event Editor for the current frame, so click the Event Editor button on the toolbar.

Highscore Frame Components

In the highscore frame, we will only do one event: If the timer is greater than 5 seconds, move to the first frame.

Timer Is Greater Than 5 Seconds

1. Click the New Condition text on event line 1. Select the Timer object and then Is the Timer Greater Than a Certain Value.

2. The Timer dialog box will appear. Type in **5** seconds and click OK.

Figure 9.15
The Storyboard Frame selector.

3. Move across to the Storyboard Controls object; then right-click and select Jump to Frame. When the Storyboard Frame selector appears, as shown in Figure 9.15, you will notice frame 1 is already selected, so click OK.

You have now completed the final frame code. Run the whole application and play your new game.

Improving the Game

There are a number of ways you could improve this game, including the following ideas:

- Create a number of levels and then change the speed of the cars and the frequency of objects, appearing to make the game harder.

- Have bonus items appear on the screen for the player to collect.

- Create a fuel level so that the player has to collect fuel to stay in the game. This adds another possibility of the game ending, rather than just relying on the player crashing.

- Add a wide array of different other vehicles on the screen.

- Create different backgrounds for the different levels; for example, a desert level, and so on.

Chapter Summary

Well done! You now have completed the third game in this book. You still have a lot to learn about the Games Factory 2, so we will now look deeper into animations, movement, and objects that can add a lot of power to your game creations. Once you have read those chapters, you will really be on your way to creating your own amazing games.

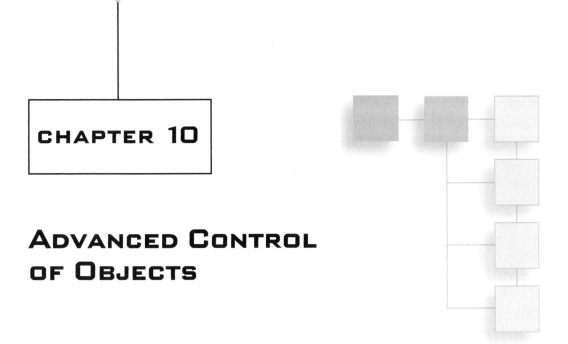

CHAPTER 10

ADVANCED CONTROL OF OBJECTS

In this chapter:

- Using Objects in Your Games
- Active Objects
- Backdrop and Quick Backdrop Objects
- Hi-Score Object
- Text Objects
- Lives Object
- Score Object
- Movement
- Chapter Summary

You may have noticed that in the previous chapters, you were never called upon to assign movement types or insert new objects. All we have done is use an already created set of game items that you placed on the frame. The next few chapters will cover ways to create and manage your own game assets. We will start by looking at Active objects and their movement, text objects, Hi-Score objects, and Backdrop objects—the mainstays of TGF2 games.

Using Objects in Your Games

TGF2 comes with a selection of objects. When creating the games in this book, you dragged these objects and placed them onto the frame from the Library Toolbar. You may have been unaware that these were all created from a basic template of objects and then configured before they were placed into the Library file from which you took them. TGF2 comes with a set of about 36 built-in objects that you can use in your creations. Common objects that you have already used, possibly without realizing it, are the Active, text, Hi-Score, and Backdrop objects.

To use an object in your games, you first have to place it on the frame. To do this, you right-click the Frame Editor and select Insert Object—or from the menu, choose Insert | New Object. You then see a list of objects to choose from, which are categorized for easier selection, as shown in Figure 10.1.

Once you have placed an object on the frame, you can configure its properties and assign it a movement type.

Figure 10.1
The selection of objects available in the TGF2 trial version.

Various objects exist for various tasks. For example, if you want to create a button, you would use a button object, or if you want video to be played in your creation, you would select the QuickTime object that would allow you to play Apple QuickTime video files.

Let's now delve into the common objects that you will use on a regular basis in your game creating.

Active Objects

Active objects are used mainly as the main characters of your games and will be the most common object used in your programs. In the games you created in earlier chapters, the objects had behaviors and movement already applied to them, so all you had to do was drag and drop them onto the frame, but when you create your own, you can assign and configure the Active Object Properties. For example, you could configure it so that the player can use the mouse or keyboard, or you can have the computer control the objects for you. You can also make your Active objects animated, making them run, jump, or do whatever you decide.

Active objects are denoted by the icon of a running man in the Create New Object dialog box and as a green diamond in the Frame Editor. The icons can be seen in Figures 10.2 and 10.3.

To place the Active object on the frame, right-click the frame, select Insert | Object, and then click Active and click OK. Finally, left-click somewhere on the frame.

You can change the object's properties by single left-clicking it and accessing the object's Properties workspace on the left-hand side, as shown in Figure 10.4.

Figure 10.2
The Active object icon in the Create New Object dialog.

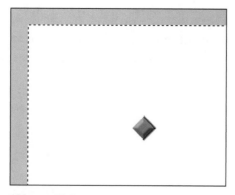

Figure 10.3
The Active object as shown in the Frame Editor.

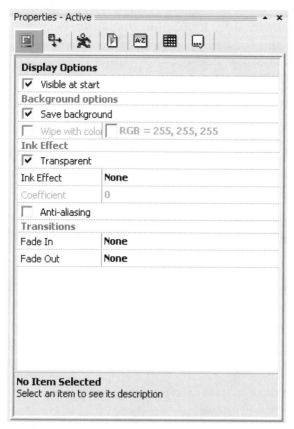

Figure 10.4
The Active Object Properties.

Don't worry about the image of the object or animation just yet, as those will be covered in the next chapter.

Every object you place on the frame can have a different set of properties. Across the top of the Properties worksheet are a number of graphical tabs that provide access to different properties from size and position to movement. Some objects have more or fewer tabs, depending on the type of object.

Text Tooltip

If you hold your mouse cursor over any of the tabs, a little Help text message will appear, telling you what each tab is.

The tabs available in this Active object are the following:

- **Display Options.** This provides different options for how the object should appear on the frame.

- **Size/Position.** What is the object's size and position on the frame? This tab is used a lot to place an object at a specific location.

- **Movement.** All objects are set to Static by default (not moving). You can specify a movement type within this tab.

- **Runtime Options.** How should the object react when the program is running?

- **Values.** You have the ability to store data of both strings (text) and numbers that are accessible to the whole application. This can be done for each object and is very useful when you are accessing the same information over each frame.

- **Events.** You can create specific events, which are stored in the selected object. This means that you can create code for how an object reacts in a certain instance and then use these objects in other TGF2 programs, and the code will still exist.

- **About.** This is your author information and the Help file link. This is very handy if you don't know what a particular option of the object does, as you can click on this Help button and read the document.

You will have used the Size/Position tab when placing objects in a specific location on the frames in previous chapters. The rest of the tabs are pretty much self-explanatory when you need to configure an object.

Backdrop and Quick Backdrop Objects

Backdrop and Quick Backdrop objects perform a similar function—to provide a background to your games. You can think of it as setting the scene in the games, where you will then place your game characters on top. A Backdrop object is usually constructed by using the Picture Editor and importing or drawing an image. You could also use one of the many backdrops provided on the CD-ROM of the full version of the software. The Picture Editor is discussed in the next chapter.

A Quick Backdrop allows you to create a background image using a selection of colors and then to use a specific shape to apply to it. You can see the icons for the Backdrop and Quick Backdrop objects in Figure 10.5.

The Backdrop object has very few properties, but under the Settings tab, you can access the Picture Editor and then draw or load a picture. The Quick Backdrop has more properties located in the Settings tab. First, you can amend the shape of the object by selecting it as a rectangle, a line, or an ellipse. When selecting the line, you can only select the color and its width, but using a rectangle or ellipse opens up a new set of options, and you can create a fill. From the Fill Type drop-down button, you can select the following options:

- **None.** This allows you to create a rectangle with a border that is configurable with a color and size. The contents of the rectangle stay with the frame color unless you change the width to a size that completely fills the shape.

Backdrop   Quick
            Backdrop

Figure 10.5
The Backdrop and Quick Backdrop object icons.

- **Solid Color.** This option fills the shape (rectangle or ellipse) with a single solid color. You can change the color by clicking the Color Settings property.

- **Gradient.** This creates a background that changes from one color to another. This is an easy way of creating a sky background, which changes color as it goes farther down the screen. If you have played old computer games, you might recognize gradients, as they were very common in games in the 1980s. To use the gradient, you normally set the first color to the darkest color you require and then set the second color to the lightest color you require. The program then creates a shape using all of the colors in between to create a background. You can set it to be a vertical or horizontal gradient by checking the Vertical Gradient button. You can see an example gradient running from black to a light red in Figure 10.6.

- **Motif.** This is the only option in the Quick Backdrop object that allows you to access the Picture Editor. The motif type takes a single image and replicates it a number of times in the Backdrop area. You can see an example of the motif in use in Figure 10.7, where a single image of a dragon has been selected, and the motif has placed it multiple times over the object.

Figure 10.6
The gradient setting used on the full size of the frame.

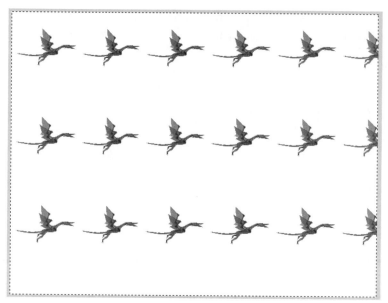

Figure 10.7
The motif setting using a dragon image on the full size of the frame.

Obstacle Type

Both the Backdrop and the Quick Backdrop objects have an additional setting under the Runtime tab. You can change how other objects interact with a Backdrop object by turning on or off the menu options in this tab under Obstacle Type. The options are shown in Figure 10.8.

There are four options:

- **None.** This option means that the Backdrop object will not be an obstacle to Active objects. You cannot detect a collision between the Backdrop object and an Active object when this option is turned on.

- **Obstacle.** This option means it is possible to detect a collision with an Active object. You must test for a collision with a Backdrop object in the Event Editor and insert a Stop action.

- **Platform.** This option means the Backdrop object acts as a platform for Active objects controlled by platform-type movement. This is not the same as the Obstacle option. You cannot detect a collision between a Backdrop object and an Active object that has been assigned a platform-type movement.

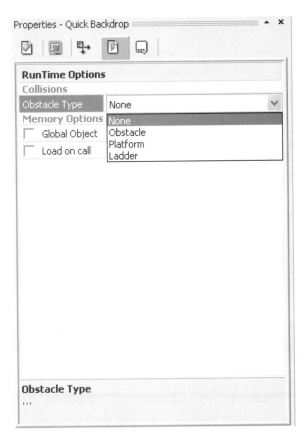

Figure 10.8
The Obstacle options.

- **Ladder.** This option treats the Backdrop object as a ladder when an Active object is using a platform-type movement. If the Active object has an animation sequence, the animation is automatically changed when the object climbs a ladder. If the Active object does not have an animation sequence, you can change the animation via the Event Editor.

Hi-Score Object

We have used the Hi-Score object a number of times in our games, where it displays the current top scores. These scores by default can contain a set of fake data for the player to try to beat, and once the player has beaten one of those scores, the Hi-Score object will also contain his score. The Hi-Score object icon is shown in Figure 10.9.

Hi-Score

Figure 10.9
The Hi-Score object icon.

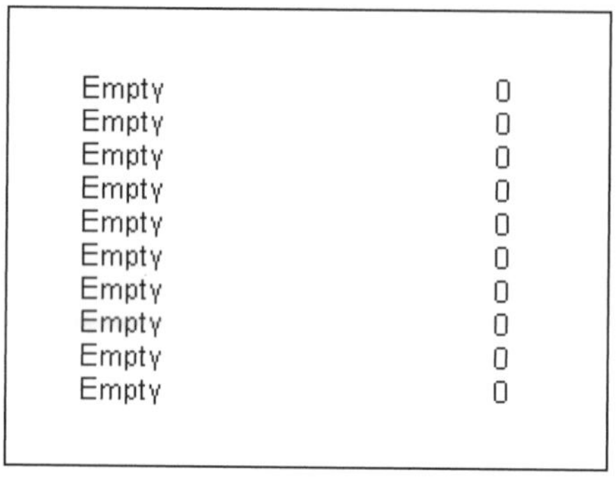

Empty	0
Empty	0
Empty	0
Empty	0
Empty	0
Empty	0
Empty	0
Empty	0
Empty	0
Empty	0

Figure 10.10
The default scoreboard.

When you place the object on the frame, you are presented with the default scoreboard, which contains 10 empty entries, as shown in Figure 10.10.

If you left-click the object, you can access the object properties. Click the Settings tab to access the key properties of this object.

Some of the options for the Hi-Score table are the following:

- **Number of Scores.** How many scores do you want to display in the Hi-Score table? The default is 10, but this is particularly useful if you only want to display a small Hi-Score table in your game.

- **Length of Names.** What length of name can the player enter when he gets a high score? If you are restricting the space that can be used for the Hi-Score table, this is useful. Additionally, if you are making a retro game, then you might be trying to replicate the three-character names that were used in many older games.

- **Show Name Before Score.** By default, the name is displayed before the score, but you can change that if required.

- **Hide at Start.** Do you want the Hi-Score table hidden at the beginning of the frame? If so, you can check this checkbox. You may want to do this if you want to control when the Hi-Score table is displayed by using code to make it reappear.

- **Check at Start.** If you want the Hi-Score table to check if the player has a top score at the start of the frame (the default), leave this checked. If, like in the games we have made, you have a separate frame for the game and the Hi-Score table, leave this checked.

- **Hide Scores.** This gives you the option of only displaying the names in the Hi-Score table.

- **Edit Content.** If you want to create a scoreboard with a set of data (recommended), you can click the Edit button to access a dialog box that allows you to put in some fake data, as shown in Figure 10.11. This is a good way to set a range of scores for the player to beat, so don't make it too easy for the player to reach the top score on his first try.

- **Name (INI file to use).** By default, the high scores are saved on the player's computer in a file called cncscore.ini in the Windows system directory. By entering a filename, you can save it in a different file.

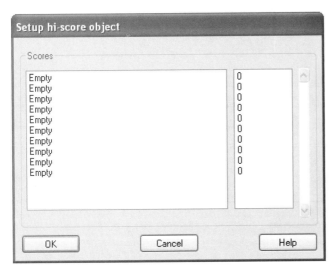

Figure 10.11
The Setup Hi-Score Object dialog box for the Hi-Score object.

Text Objects

Text objects are used to put text on the screen. You can use them for instructions, comments, end-of-game displays, or just about anything that requires text. It is very easy to make your own text once you have placed a text object on the frame from the Add Object dialog.

There are three text-based objects in TGF2:

- Formatted text

- Static text

- String

You can see the object icons for all three of these objects in Figure 10.12.

Available in all three objects is the ability to select fonts, styles, text sizes, and text color, as well as the justification style you want to use. The Formatted Text object allows you to access these features via the toolbar, and you can access the Static Text and String objects via the Object Properties worksheet, as shown in Figures 10.13 and 10.14.

Formatted Text   Static Text   String

Figure 10.12
The three text-based objects available in TGF2.

Figure 10.13
The Font options on the toolbar.

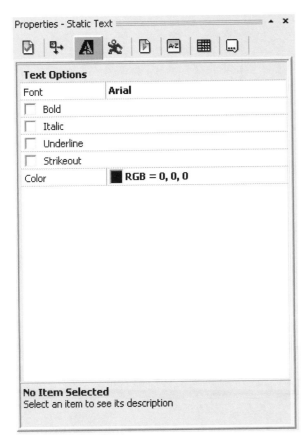

Figure 10.14
The Font options in the Properties sheet.

Lives Object

The Lives object is for keeping track of a player's lives in the game. The icon in the Add Object dialog can be seen in Figure 10.15.

Once placed on the Frame Editor, it appears as three hearts, as shown in Figure 10.16. This means the player has three lives, which is the default setting for the Lives object.

Lives

Figure 10.15
The Lives object in the Add Object dialog box.

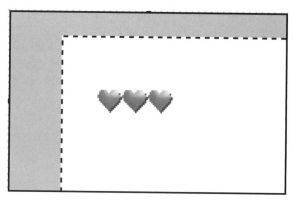

Figure 10.16
The Lives object, as displayed on the Frame Editor.

To use the Lives object within the context of your game, you need to use the Event Editor.

Default Number of Lives

If you want to change the default number of lives from three to another number, you need to click the application name and then click the Runtime Options tab for the Application Properties. Under the Players heading, you then have access to the initial number of Lives option.

The Settings tab of the Lives object can be seen in Figure 10.17 and has only three key settings:

■ **Player.** Which player do these lives images apply to? If you are creating a game with multiple players, for example, a two-player game, you can specify which player these belong to.

■ **Type.** You can change the display of the Lives object by selecting one of the three options in the Type drop-down box. The default is Image, which displays a heart graphic. You can also select Text or Numbers. You can also edit the image option and replace it with your own Lives image.

■ **Image(s).** This button allows you to access the Picture Editor and change the look of the Lives object.

Score Object

The Score object is used to keep track of the current player's score in the game. You can see the Score object icon, as shown in the Add Object dialog box in Figure 10.18.

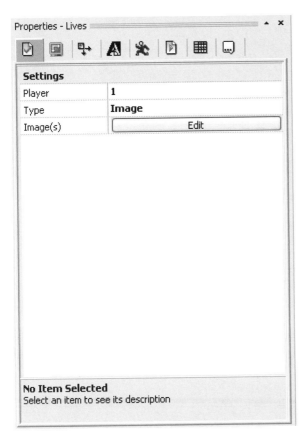

Figure 10.17
The Settings tab of the Lives object.

Score

Figure 10.18
The Score object icon in the Add Object dialog.

Once you have added the icon to the desktop, it will automatically be displayed as a graphic number 0. The Settings tab of the Object Properties has the same set of options as the Lives object.

Movement

To change an object's movement from the Frame Editor, left-click the object to display the Object Properties and then click the Movement tab in the Properties workspace. You will see the current Movement options for this Active object, as shown in Figure 10.19.

Figure 10.19
The Movement tab in the Object Properties sheet.

Nearly every type of object in TGF2 can be assigned a movement, and though we are discussing it within the context of applying it to an Active object, the process and options are the same for any other object.

Notice that the Movement type of the object is currently set to Static. This is the default setting of all objects when they are created from the Insert | New Object menu. By clicking Static, you reveal all of the available Movement types, as shown in Figure 10.20.

Additional Movements

More Movement types are available in the full version of TGF2 after the latest patch has been installed.

There are three computer-controlled options: Bouncing Ball, Path, and Pinball Movement. There are four types of movement that can be used by the player of

Figure 10.20
The available Movement types in the trial version.

the game when controlling what is happening on-screen: Mouse Controlled, Eight Directions, Race Car, and Platform.

We will now go through each of these Movement types so you have a better understanding of what they do and how you apply them to objects.

Bouncing Ball

This Movement option, as shown in Figure 10.21, is normally used to produce an object that bounces around the screen like a ball. However, by changing several parameters and using the Event Editor, you can use this movement to control the movement of a host of aliens or other enemies that chase the player around. You can see the other key settings of the Movement tab for the Bouncing Ball in Figure 10.22.

Figure 10.21
The Bouncing Ball icon.

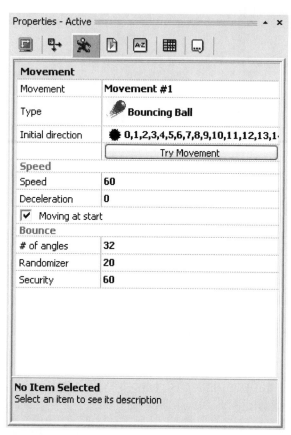

Figure 10.22
The Movement tab for the Bouncing Ball movement.

Initial direction defines which direction the object moves when the game first starts. The numbers relate to a direction—for example, 8 is up and 0 is to the right. You can click the numbers to reveal a direction chart, where you can remove or add check marks to tell TGF2 which directions the object is able to

Figure 10.23
The Initial Direction dialog.

move. You can see the Initial Direction dialog in Figure 10.23. Here are some direction parameters that you can define:

- **Speed.** Speed controls the speed of all the other types of movement.

- **Ball Deceleration.** When this option is set to zero, a ball keeps bouncing forever. Increasing this value gradually slows your object down until it grinds to a halt.

- **Moving at Start.** The object moves automatically when the game starts. If you uncheck this option, you need to start the object moving via the Event Editor.

- **# of Angles.** Number of angles lets you set the bounce angle for the object. It can be 32, 16, or 8. The fewer angles selected, the fewer directions the ball will bounce.

- **Randomizer.** This option makes objects bounce in more random directions. As this number increases, so does the randomness.

- **Security.** This option jiggles objects to keep them from getting stuck in corners, but as a result, the rebound effects are made slightly more random.

Figure 10.24
The Path icon.

Figure 10.25
The Path Editor option buttons.

Path

The Path option shown in Figure 10.24 sets your object moving on a pre-determined path, which you define. For example, you can create a patrolling guard who walks a set distance and then turns around or who walks in a preset path around a corridor. This lets you control many parameters and script some neat effects, such as the looping and speed that an object will move with on different sections of its path.

To access the options for the Path, click Edit.

As shown in Figure 10.25, six buttons let you define the movement of an object, plus the Speed Bar, which changes the speed at which the object moves along its path. A path-type movement is entered using your mouse to define the path.

Here are the six buttons to define movement, plus a few other options:

- **New Line.** This function adds a single line to the object's movement.

New Line

If you already have a movement defined, New Line is added at the end of it by default, unless you insert it somewhere else by choosing the insertion point with the mouse.

- **Tape Mouse.** This function allows you to set a very complex path movement. By holding down the left mouse button and dragging the mouse pointer around the screen, you set the movement you want.

■ **Pause.** This function stops your object at its current position for a length of time that you define in seconds.

■ **Loop the Movement.** This function repeats a movement that you specify, over and over.

Looping Path Movement

Each time the loop repeats, this function repositions the object back to its original starting position, so make sure the path finishes at the object's starting point, or the object will jump around the screen.

■ **Reverse at End.** This function reverses an object's movement and sends it backward along the original path. This function is good for a guard patrolling the grounds.

■ **Reposition Object at End.** This function puts your object back at its original starting position when it has completed the movement.

■ **Try Movement.** This function lets you try the movement before deciding upon it.

■ **Editing a Path.** Once you have added a movement to your object, you can edit it very easily in the Frame Editor. To do this, select the object, choose the Movement tab in the Object Properties Toolbar, and click Edit. This opens the Path Editor again. You can select individual points of the movement, or you can choose entire sections by dragging a box around them. You can manipulate these selected pieces by either deleting them or using the Cut (CTRL-X), Copy (CTRL-C), and Paste (CTRL-V) keys. You can also simply drag one of the selected areas using the left mouse button.

Path Nodes

Each box created on the path movement is called a *node*.

■ **Configuring Node Properties.** After you've selected a point or area, you can add a condition to it by right-clicking any node in the path. This lets you insert a condition at that spot, such as Set a Pause, Tape Mouse, or New Line. You can see the pop-up menu when you right-click a node in Figure 10.26.

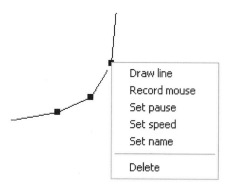

Figure 10.26
Add a condition by right-clicking a node.

Figure 10.27
The icon for the Pinball movement.

Pinball Movement

This allows you to create a movement similar to the bouncing ball movement, but the ball reacts as if it were in a pinball machine. You can see the icon for this movement in Figure 10.27 and the properties in Figure 10.28.

The Pinball properties are as follows:

- **Gravity.** This option selects the effect of gravity. A high setting makes your object fall rapidly, allowing only short bounces.

- **Deceleration.** Deceleration sets the rate at which your object slows down.

- **Move at Start.** When checked, the Move at Start option causes the object to move in one of the directions you have chosen when the game starts. When this option is unchecked, the object remains stationary until told to move via the Event Editor.

- **Initial Speed.** This is the initial starting speed of the object.

- **Initial Direction.** This option allows you to choose one or more directions for your object to move when the game begins. If you choose more than one direction, TGF2 chooses one of the specified directions at random.

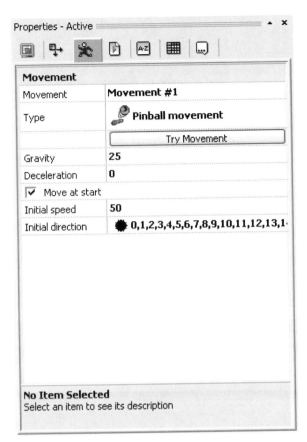

Figure 10.28
The Properties sheet for the Pinball movement.

Figure 10.29
The Mouse Controlled icon.

Mouse Controlled

The first type of player-controlled movement is Mouse Controlled. This makes the object follow the movement of the mouse exactly. The icon for this object can be seen in Figure 10.29. To edit the area where the mouse can move, click the Edit box. The object will be surrounded by a box that represents the object's limits of movement, as shown in Figure 10.30.

You can stretch or shrink the area by grabbing the sizing handles with your mouse and dragging them around.

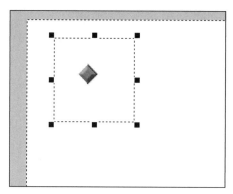

Figure 10.30
The Mouse Movement area control box.

Mouse Controlled Box

This box takes its position from the object, not from the screen. This means that if you move the object to a new position on the Frame Editor screen, you may need to edit this box again.

Try Movement tests your object's movement on the screen. To stop the object and return to the Mouse Controlled dialog, press the Escape key.

Eight Directions

This movement control, whose icon is shown in Figure 10.31, provides you with the classic eight directions that are used by a joystick. You can also use the cursor keys to control movement. There are several basic controls. Speed, Acceleration, and Deceleration have been described previously. The Possible Directions option allows you to select or deselect the number of directions in which your object can move. See Figure 10.32 for the Movement Direction dialog Properties sheet and Figure 10.33 for the Direction and Initial Directions dialog.

To select or deselect a direction, click the relevant box (either Direction or Initial Direction). Having an arrow pointing to that box shows its possible directions. In Figure 10.33, the object can move in eight directions. You can click the button on

Figure 10.31
The Eight Directions icon.

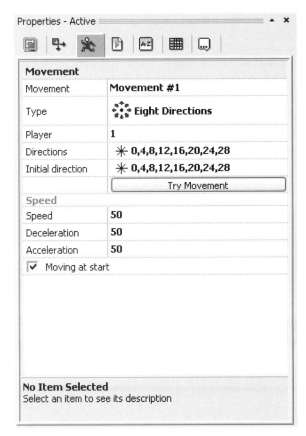

Figure 10.32
The Movement Direction Properties sheet.

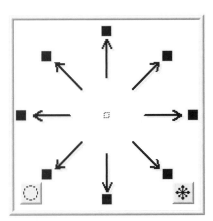

Figure 10.33
Direction and Initial Direction have the same dialog.

Figure 10.34
The Race Car icon.

Figure 10.35
The Race Car Properties sheet.

the bottom-left side of the Direction dialog to remove all directions so you can place one or more directions manually. If you click the icon on the bottom-right side of the Direction dialog, it selects all directions.

Race Car

Figure 10.34 shows the icon for the Race Car movement, and Figure 10.35 shows its Properties sheet. This movement type simulates a bird's-eye view of a car's movement. There are controls for steering, braking, and accelerating, which users can activate by pressing a key or using a joystick. You can see the keys that can be used for this movement in Table 10.1.

Table 10.1 Keys Used for Race Car Movement

Action	Keyboard
Accelerate	Up arrow
Brake	Down arrow
Turn left	Left arrow
Turn right	Right arrow

In addition to the Speed, Acceleration, and Deceleration settings are three more important options:

- **Enable Reverse.** This option gives your object the ability to go backward. With it turned off, the object can only move forward.

- **# of Angles.** This allows you to decide how many different directions the object can move. Selecting four only gives you left, right, up, and down; selecting 32 gives you the smoothest possible direction changes.

Animation Directions

You can easily create all the different animation needed for each direction by using the Animation tool available in the Picture Editor. We will discuss this feature in the next chapter.

- **Rotating Speed.** Rotating Speed sets the rate at which the object turns. A high value allows tight corners to be turned, while a low value reduces the cornering ability.

Platform

This movement icon in Figure 10.36 and its Properties sheet in Figure 10.37 are used to define platform-game type movement. This means characters walk along a set of platforms and climb ladders or jump between floors, viewed from the side, as in games such as Commander Keen and Zeb. Movement is controlled by the cursor keys or the joystick. In addition to the usual Acceleration, Deceleration, and Speed controls are a number of controls for jumping. You can make platforms and ladders out of backdrop objects.

⬛🔧 **Platform**

Figure 10.36
The Platform icon.

Figure 10.37
The Platform movement Properties sheet.

Testing for Collisions

You must still test for a collision with a backdrop Platform object; otherwise, your Active object will fall through the platform as if it weren't there. You can do this through the Event Editor.

The properties for the Platform movement are as follows:

- **Initial Direction.** This option allows you to choose one or more directions for your object to move when the game begins. If you choose more than one direction, TGF2 will choose one of the specified directions at random.

- **Try Movement.** You can test out the movement on-screen, without the need to leave the Movement Editing screen.

- **Speed.** This option sets the maximum speed at which your object can move.

- **Acceleration.** Acceleration sets the rate at which your object speeds up to its maximum speed.

- **Deceleration.** Deceleration sets the rate at which your character object slows down.

- **Moving at Start.** When checked, the Moving at Start option causes the object to move in one of the directions you have chosen when the game starts. When this option is unchecked, the object remains stationary until another object collides with it.

- **Gravity.** This option selects the effect of gravity. A high setting makes your object fall rapidly, allowing only short jumps.

- **Strength.** Jump Strength selects the jumping power of your character. Changing the gravity also affects this parameter.

- **Jump Controls.** Jump Controls are used to change the control system for jumps, as follows.

    - *No Jump.* This option turns jumping off for an object.

    - *Up Left/Right Arrow.* This option makes the object jump when the up arrow key is pressed at the same time as either the left arrow or right arrow key.

    - *Button 1.* Button 1 uses Fire button one, or the Shift key, to control the jump.

    - *Button 2.* Button 2 uses the second Fire button, or the Control key, to activate a jump.

Multiple Movements

In all of the movement types, you may have noticed that the very first option in the Properties sheets, which we didn't cover, is just displayed as Movement #1. This is the default first movement assigned to that Movement type. In TGF2, you can assign multiple movement types to a single object, so you could create three movements for your character: the first being Platform, the second being Race Car, and the third being Mouse Controlled. Of course, this is unlikely in most cases, but when making games it does give you a lot of flexibility to control the objects in your game. An example of this might be that you create a side-scrolling

Figure 10.38
The multiple Movements dialog.

game in which the player controls the character using the Platform movement. Perhaps at a certain stage, you switch off the Platform movement and assign a Path movement to move the player's character to a specific position to allow for your game to tell a story. By doing this, you can prevent the player from moving the character, and you can tell this part of the story. Perhaps in this case, another computer-controlled player appears and says something to the game player's character. You can then switch back to the Platform movement and allow the player to continue with the game.

To access the multiple movements, click Movement #1, and you will see a + − button. Click this to display the Movements dialog, as shown in Figure 10.38.

From here, you can create new movements and go back into the properties of the object and select the movement number and change the movement type. You can also rename the movement to something more appropriate.

Chapter Summary

In this chapter, we looked at the basis for all TGF2 games: the Active objects, Backdrops, text, Hi-Score, Lives, and Score objects. These are the most common Active objects in TGF2, and the ones you will be working with the most. In the next chapter, we will look at asset creation using the Picture Editor. These tools will round out your ability to make your own games and productions with TGF2.

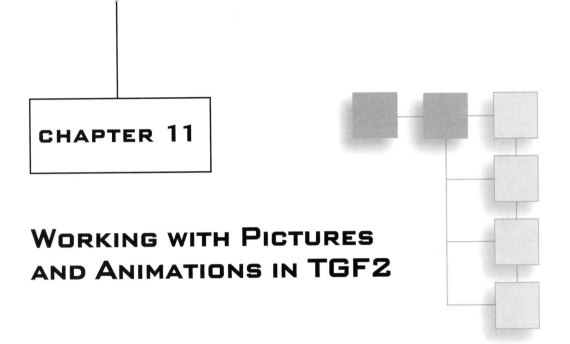

CHAPTER 11

WORKING WITH PICTURES AND ANIMATIONS IN TGF2

In this chapter:

- The Picture Editor

- The Animation Tool

- Chapter Summary

We will look at how to create and manipulate assets for your games. One of the most useful tools for the game developer that comes with TGF2 is the Picture Editor. This editor makes it easy to import and deal with your game assets. This includes animation functions that previously required you to work manually in another application, such as Photoshop, including copying, rotating, and performing other tedious operations.

The Picture Editor

The Picture Editor lets you create your own animation, Background objects, icons, and Quick Backdrop objects. Because many of the features are identical for all these types of objects, they are summarized in this chapter.

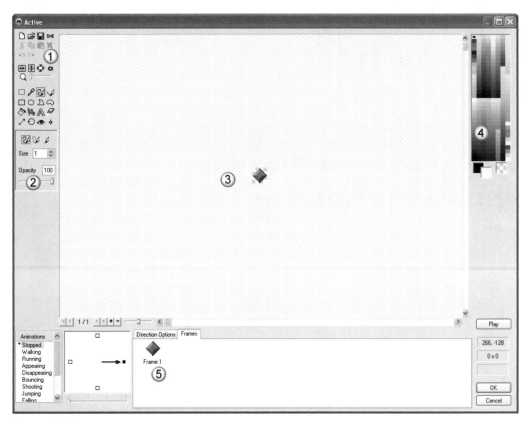

Figure 11.1
The TGF2 Picture Editor.

You can see the Picture Editor in Figure 11.1, as well as the other components that make up the editor, which include:

1. Tools

2. Tool Properties sheet

3. Drawing area

4. Color Palette

5. Animation Editor

Tools

The drawing tools are located at the upper left of the Picture Editor window. They include the most commonly used features of the digital artist in other paint

Figure 11.2
The Clear option.

Figure 11.3
The Import option icon.

packages. We will now look at the various tools that make up the Picture Editor's toolbox, starting from the top left and working to the right.

Clear

This option clears the image window so you can start from scratch. If you accidentally clear work that you wanted to save, you can undo the Clear command by clicking the Cancel button and re-editing the image or using the hot key combination Ctrl+Z. You can see the icon for the Clear option in Figure 11.2.

Import

This tool allows you to load an image from a disk; the associated icon is shown in Figure 11.3. As the picture and animation aspects work hand in hand, you can import multiple pictures at a time to save time. The import supports the following:

- PNG

- JPEG

- GIF

- FLC

- BMP

- PCX

To use the Import option, you need to select the file you want to import (if you want to import multiple files, select the first one of its type). An Import Options dialog box appears, providing you with different options to configure your import selection, as shown in Figure 11.4.

Some of the import features are discussed in a bit more detail later in this chapter.

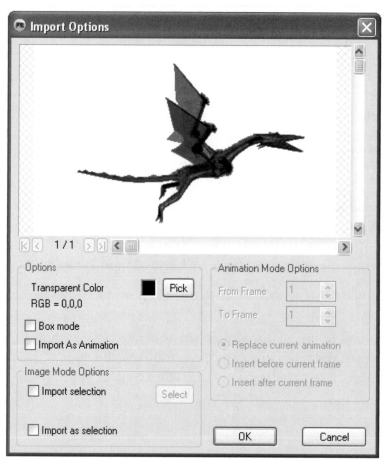

Figure 11.4
The Import Options dialog.

Figure 11.5
The Export option icon.

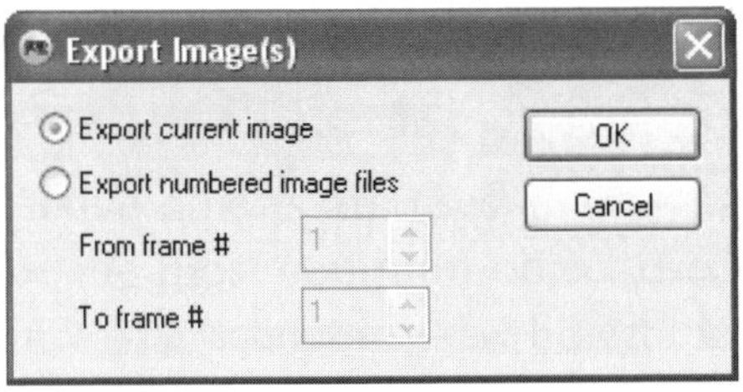

Figure 11.6
The Export Image(s) dialog.

Export

Export allows you to save any file you have been working on into a stand-alone file. When you create a picture from scratch in TGF2's Picture Editor, you can only access it through TGF2. By using the Export option, you can save the file and its animations to an external file(s) that can then be accessible by another paint program. The Export option allows you to save the files as PNG, BMP, or JPG files. The Export icon can be seen in Figure 11.5.

When you click the Export button, you will be given a simple dialog to select if you want to export a single file or an animation with a number of frames, as shown in Figure 11.6.

Options

Options allow you to configure how the right mouse button is utilized in the Picture Editor. It is common for the right mouse button to be assigned to a second color so you can use two colors at one time without needing to swap between them. This is particularly helpful when you are doing fine art and might be using two similar colors at one time. You can configure the right mouse button to select the color of the pixel where the mouse cursor is situated. You can also configure the background display where there is no image, which by default is gray and white. The icon for the Options can be seen in Figure 11.7, and the associated Picture Editor Preferences dialog box can be seen in Figure 11.8.

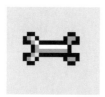

Figure 11.7
The Options icon.

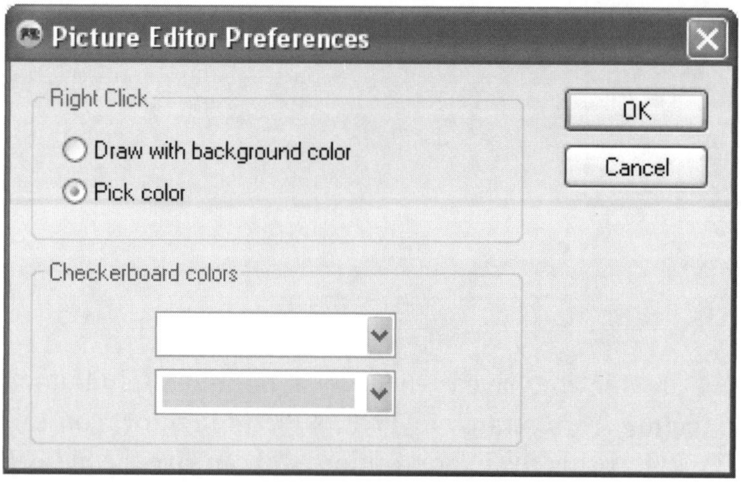

Figure 11.8
The Picture Editor Preferences dialog.

Figure 11.9
The Cut, Copy, Paste, and Delete icons.

Cut, Copy, Paste, and Delete

Once you have selected a block on the canvas, you can cut and copy it using the following commands from various buttons, as shown in Figure 11.9.

■ **Cut.** The original area is cut out and replaced with a block of whatever the transparency color currently is. A copy of that area is placed on the Windows clipboard.

- **Copy.** The area is copied to the Windows clipboard. The original area remains unchanged.

- **Paste.** Pastes the contents of the Windows clipboard. After you have cut an area, you can copy it onto the image using this command. The pasted area is in a rectangular block. Drag this block where you want it and then click it to fix it in place.

- **Delete.** Deletes the contents of the selected area.

Undo and Redo

The Undo tool lets you undo the last step you performed. This is very handy if you make a mistake. If you change your mind when you have undone something, you can click the Redo icon to change it back. You can see the Undo and Redo icons in Figure 11.10.

Flip Horizontally

This tool reverses your image from left to right, just like a mirror.

Flip Vertically

This tool turns the whole image upside down. The icons for both Flip Horizontally and Flip Vertically can be seen in Figure 11.11.

Figure 11.10
The Undo and Redo icons.

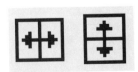

Figure 11.11
The Flip Horizontally and Flip Vertically icons.

Crop

Crop removes any available blank space on the canvas. If you have a large canvas, and only a small part of it has any image on it, the Picture Editor tries to remove as much of the blank space as it can by using straight lines. The Crop icon can be seen in Figure 11.12.

Transparency

Transparency allows you to display the transparent color, but it also allows you to change it quickly by clicking the Color Palette. You can then hide the transparent color again by unchecking the box. The Transparency button and its Properties box can be seen in Figures 11.13 and 11.14.

Figure 11.12
The Crop icon.

Figure 11.13
The Transparency icon.

Figure 11.14
The Transparency Properties box.

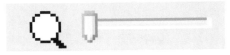

Figure 11.15
The Zoom Control.

Figure 11.16
The Selection tool icon.

Zoom Control

The Zoom Control, as shown in Figure 11.15, allows you to zoom in closer or zoom out of the current image. If the slider is to the left, it is zoomed out to the maximum canvas size. The farther it is to the right, the higher the zoom magnification is.

The Selection Tool

This tool lets you define a rectangular block, which you can then cut or copy. To choose a block, move the mouse to where you want the top-left corner of your block to be and then drag a box down around the area you want. If you make a mistake, click once on another part of your image and try again. You can see the Selection icon in Figure 11.16.

Color Picker

The Color Picker allows you to click anywhere on the canvas and change the current pen color to the selected color. This is very useful when you want to pick a pen color that is already in use on the canvas rather than trying to guess exactly what the color is. You can see the Color Picker icon in Figure 11.17.

The Pen Tool

The Pen tool lets you either draw one pixel at a time or draw a freehand line by holding down the left mouse button and dragging over the canvas. You can see the Pen icon in Figure 11.18.

Figure 11.17
The Color Picker icon.

Figure 11.18
The Pen tool icon.

Figure 11.19
The Line tool icon.

The Line Tool

The Line tool lets you draw perfect straight lines. Click the point where you want the line to start and hold down the mouse button. As you move the mouse, it "drags" a line behind it. When you reach the place where you want the line to end, let go of the mouse button, and you will have drawn a line between the two points. You can see the Line tool icon in Figure 11.19.

The Rectangle and Filled Rectangle Tools

These tools and their Properties boxes let you draw rectangles and squares more easily than by trying to construct them out of four separate lines. After selecting

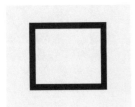

Figure 11.20
The Rectangle tool icon.

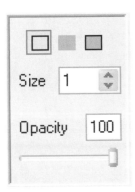

Figure 11.21
The Rectangle tool properties.

the icon you want, place the pointer where you want the top-left corner, press and hold down the mouse button, and then drag the rectangle to the shape you want. The Rectangle tool produces an unfilled (clear) rectangle. You can select one of the alternative options in the Properties box (shown as option 2 in Figure 11.1) to either produce a solid rectangle or a solid rectangle with a different border color. You can see the Rectangle icon and its properties in Figures 11.20 and 11.21.

The Ellipse and Filled Ellipse Tools

These tools and their Properties sheets let you create ellipses and circles, both filled and empty. Select the place where you want to start the top-left side of the ellipse. Hold down the mouse button and move the pointer away from the place you first began the ellipse. You can see the Ellipse icon and its Properties sheet in Figures 11.22 and 11.23.

Figure 11.22
The Ellipse button icon.

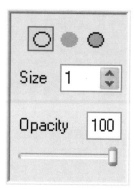

Figure 11.23
The Ellipse Properties window.

Figure 11.24
The Polygon button icon.

Polygon Tool

It is very simple to create a polygon shape using this tool. You can draw a number of lines that connect to each other. You can see the Polygon tool icon in Figure 11.24 and its Properties sheet in Figure 11.25.

A polygon is a shape made up of straight lines, so a square, rectangle, and triangle can all be considered polygons. These shapes are made easier to create in the size and shape you want using this tool.

Figure 11.25
The Properties sheet for the Polygon tool.

Figure 11.26
The Shape tool icon.

Figure 11.27
The Shape tool Properties sheet.

Shape Tool

The Shape tool allows you to draw a shape, and it will completely enclose it, so if you begin to draw a circle but take your finger off the left mouse button while drawing it, the program completely closes the shape. This allows you to fill the item with a color, if required. You can see the Shape tool icon in Figure 11.26 and its Properties sheet in Figure 11.27.

Figure 11.28
The Fill tool icon.

Figure 11.29
The Fill tool Properties sheet.

The Fill Tool

The Fill tool fills an area on the canvas with a solid block of color. The area to be filled should be completely enclosed. If there is a gap of even one pixel, the color will "leak" out into other areas of your frame. In Figures 11.28 and 11.29 you can see the Fill icon and its Properties sheet.

The Spray Tool

This works the same way a spray can works. It applies a spray of paint onto the canvas. You can change the size of the paint pixel and the pressure that's applied. This works in very much the same way as using a can of paint, where the longer you apply it to a specific area of the wall (or in this case the canvas), the more paint it will apply.

You can see the icon for the Spray tool in Figure 11.30 and its Properties sheet in Figure 11.31.

Figure 11.30
The Spray tool icon.

Figure 11.31
The Spray tool Properties sheet.

Figure 11.32
The Text tool icon.

The Text Tool

This allows you to place a piece of text, either a single letter or words, on the canvas. You can apply basic formatting to the text, including bold, italic, and underline. It is also possible to select a specific font for the text. You can see the icon for the Text tool in Figure 11.32 and its Properties sheet in Figure 11.33.

Eraser Tool

This tool allows you to delete a part of your picture, basically rubbing it out. You can amend the eraser size for when you need to delete a large amount of the

Figure 11.33
The Text tool Properties sheet.

Figure 11.34
The Eraser icon.

Figure 11.35
The Size icon.

image or area on the canvas, or you can make the eraser very small for more precise deletions by selecting a smaller eraser shape in the Paint Toolbox. You can see the Eraser tool icon in Figure 11.34.

Size

This allows you to change the size of the image on the canvas. Its icon can be seen in Figure 11.35. There are also three additional options to stretch the image, to resample it, and make it proportional to the canvas size. This Properties sheet can be seen in Figure 11.36.

Figure 11.36
The Size Properties sheet.

Figure 11.37
The Rotate icon.

Figure 11.38
The Rotate Properties sheet.

Rotate

This tool lets you rotate the whole image with fine control. When you select this function, you can enter a specific angle by which to rotate the image on the Properties sheet. Once you have clicked OK, the image is turned by the angle you specified. The icon for the Rotate option and its properties can be seen in Figures 11.37 and 11.38.

Figure 11.39
The Hot Spot icon.

Figure 11.40
The Hot Spot Properties sheet.

View Hot Spot

The Hot Spot is an invisible handle, or anchor, that you can use to drag images around the screen. It is also used as a reference for an object's x, y-coordinates. Each image can have its own separate Hot Spot. As a default, when you create a new active object, the Hot Spot is automatically positioned at the top-left corner of the image, but you can move it anywhere you like.

You can view the Hot Spot by selecting the View Hot Spot icon. Try to position it centrally if your object is going to have several different directions; otherwise, it will "jump" when you change direction. You can see the Hot Spot icon and its Properties sheet in Figures 11.39 and 11.40.

View Action Point

The Action Point is the point where things like bullets are fired from objects. For example, if you had a large spaceship with a gun mounted on it, you would set the Action Point to the end of the gun barrel, where the bullet would first appear. You can show the Action Point by clicking the View Action Point button. You

Figure 11.41
The Action Point icon.

can see the Action Point icon in Figure 11.41. Its Properties sheet looks exactly like the Hot Spot Properties sheet in Figure 11.40.

Drawing Area

There's not much to say about the drawing area. This is the place where you draw your images. If your image is too large for the window, horizontal and vertical scroll bars allow you to move around.

The Color Palette

This is where you select the color you want to draw or fill the canvas with. Figure 11.42 shows a selection of colors to choose from when drawing. The two boxes on the bottom left are the current draw colors for the left and right mouse buttons. The box on the bottom right is the currently selected transparent color.

The Animation Tool

Animation is a word that still strikes fear in the hearts of many who want to develop games, but TGF2 makes animation a lot easier with its Animation tools built into the Picture Editor. When using the Picture Editor and its Animation tools:

- You can create your own Active object, draw or import images, and animate them.

- You can use an already created Active object, which already contains animations, and then change or update it.

To show you some of the animation features, you will be using a TGF2 file that has an Active object that already exists on the frame and analyzing how the tools have been used to animate it. As you do this, you will see the steps required to create your own animated object.

Figure 11.42
The Color Palette.

1. You need to have TGF2 loaded with no file currently loaded.

2. Click File | Open and browse the CD-ROM provided with this book and locate the file called dragonanimation.mfa, which is in the TGFFILES folder. Then click Open to load it into the program.

3. Double left-click frame 1 to open the Frame Editor.

4. Notice an Active object of a dragon is already on the playfield. Click Run Application to see the dragon fly, as shown in Figure 11.43.

5. This Active object is moving because it already has its animation applied to it. To see this, you need to enter the Picture Editor and view its frames in the Animation tool, so double left-click the dragon picture.

Figure 11.43
Animated Active object of a dragon.

6. You can now see the dragon in the canvas area and all of its animation frames in the Animation tool, as shown in Figure 11.44.

You can see the different sections of the Animation tool, as separated in Figure 11.45.

The different sections for the Animation tool are as follows:

1. These are all the available animations that you can place images against. You can also create your own animation groups.

2. These are the available directions each animation can have. Initially this is set to four directions, but you can use the slider underneath it to increase it to 32 directions.

3. This is the Frame Tools bar, where you can add frames and move through the available frames you have created. This updates the current frame being displayed on the canvas.

4. These are all of the frames of your animation for this particular animation group.

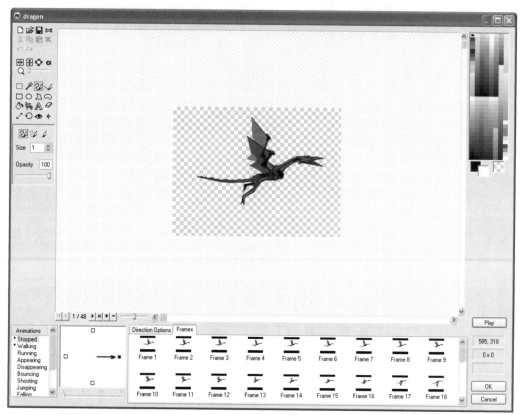

Figure 11.44
The animation frames for the dragon.

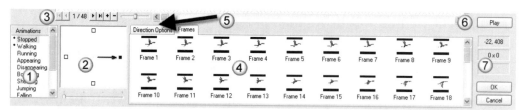

Figure 11.45
Various areas of the animation tool.

5. The Direction Options tab contains specific information relating to the speed of the animation and its loops.

6. This plays the current animation to give you an idea of what it looks like.

7. This provides information about the cursor position on the canvas and the colors in use at that particular pixel.

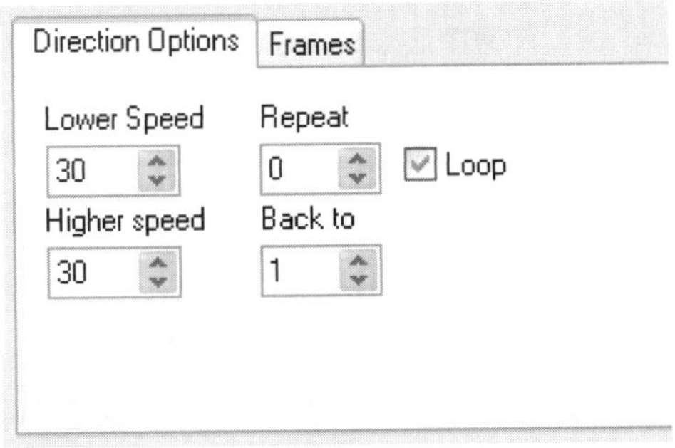

Figure 11.46
The Direction Options tab.

Selecting Animation Frames

To select all the frames of an animation, press Alt+A once you have single left-clicked in the Animation Frame window. This lets you move or delete a whole sequence of animations at one time. You can select multiple frames by holding down the Ctrl key while you click frames, or hold down the Shift key to select all frames between two selected frames.

Directions Tab

Figure 11.46 shows the controls for the speed of the animation (the Lower and Higher Speed boxes), as well as the number of times it will repeat itself before it stops (the Repeat box). You can select looping by checking the Loop box. This makes the animation sequence repeat over and over.

You can also change which frame number the animation loops back to in the Back To box. This is useful in a long animation if you only want to repeat certain parts. Say you are working with an animation of a man getting up from a crouched position and then running away. You may only want to play the first couple of frames of him being crouched down and then loop the animation back only to the running sequence as the man continues running.

Animation Speeds

An animation can have either one or two speeds assigned to it. An object can be animated but be static with regard to its location on-screen, or it can be animated and move around the screen. The difference is that the second scenario also has a movement speed assigned to it, as well as its animated speed.

Lower Speed

The Lower Speed box in the Direction Options tab controls the speed when the character is not moving around the screen. Setting this to zero halts the animation.

Setting it higher has the animation running all of the time. Of course, it may look unrealistic if your character is running frantically without moving.

Higher Speed

The Higher Speed box in the Direction Options tab controls the maximum rate of the animation when the character is moving around the screen. Note that the rate of animation is proportional to the speed of the character in between the Lower and Higher settings. To create a realistic running action, you may need to change the Higher setting to a value that matches the character's speed across the screen. For example, if you were to set a character's movement speed high and the animation speed low, it would appear as though the character were being dragged across the screen. If you had the animation speed high and the movement speed low, it would look as though the character were trying to run fast on an icy floor.

Animation Direction

This is a very useful feature that can transform your single-direction animation into a character that moves to the left, right, up, down, and so on. Take a look at the Direction box, as shown in Figure 11.47, where two images show the left and right directions of our flying dragon. By clicking the different direction squares in the Direction box, you can create a different animation for each direction the character can move.

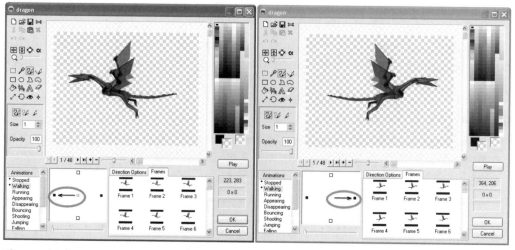

Figure 11.47
The difference between the left and right direction arrows.

If you take a look at Figure 11.47, you can see that on the clock face, the 3 o'clock position (rightward motion) and the 9 o'clock position (leftward motion) have small solid black squares with arrows pointing to them. These indicate that an animation is assigned to those positions, so the dragon has different animations for going left and right.

Counting all possible directions, you can have up to 32 animated sequences for the walk direction of a character. This can help things look smooth, but it is overkill for most purposes. As computers have become more powerful, selecting 32 directions wouldn't cause too much of a resource issue. In a large game with many directions and animations, it would start to add up, and, although in most cases this wouldn't slow your machine down, it's good to get into good habits when creating your games. Why waste resources if you don't need to? In the case of the flying dragon, you only need to move it left and right, so there is no need to select 32 directions when you are only going to use 2.

Creating Copies of Animations

An easy way to create several different directions from one animation is to copy the animation to the new direction and then click the Rotate buttons to ensure that it is pointing the correct way.

Animations List

The default Animations list can be seen in Figure 11.48. This list details the basic set of animations provided with TGF2 that can have animations placed within them. These animations can be referenced from within the Event Editor, but they

Figure 11.48
The Animations list.

also work automatically when using certain movement types on that particular object. The animation sets are the following:

- **Stopped.** When the object is not moving.

- **Walking.** Checks the speed of an object and runs this animation if it is moving at a slow pace.

- **Running.** Checks the speed of an object and runs this animation if it is moving at a fast pace.

- **Appearing.** Runs the animation as soon as the object is created.

- **Disappearing.** Runs the animation as soon as the object is destroyed.

- **Bouncing.** Plays the animation when the object is bouncing on another object that is defined as an obstacle (something that it will bounce or hit).

- **Shooting.** The animation is triggered when a shoot object is triggered.

- **Jumping.** The animation is played when the object is jumping. Jumping is used in platform movement games.

- **Falling.** When an object is falling, the animation is played. This animation is used primarily in platform games.

- **Climbing.** When using the platform movement, this animation plays when the object is climbing a ladder.

- **Crouch Down.** If you are using platform movement, this animation set runs when the object is crouching.

- **Stand up.** When the object is standing up (not crouching), this animation runs. This is also used in platform movement for platform games.

You can create your own animation sets for anything that is not covered in this list. These are called *user-defined animations*. To create your own animation set, right-click the Animations list and select New. You can then enter the name of the animation set.

Chapter Summary

In this chapter, we have taken a look at how to use and create your own game graphic assets. To do this, you can use another paint package and then import images into TGF2, or you can draw them inside the program's Picture Editor. Either way, you should have enough knowledge to be able to attempt it in TGF2. You should now be able to begin creating and designing your own 2D games in TGF2. If you need any help, you can consult the Help file in the Help | Contents menu.

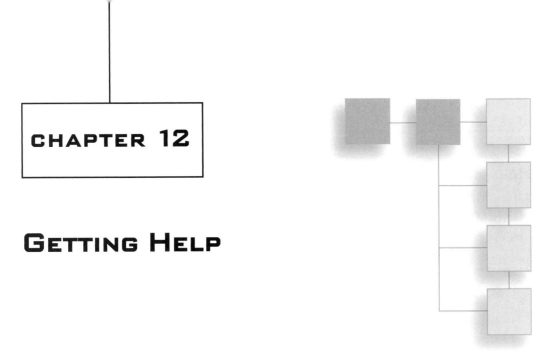

CHAPTER 12

GETTING HELP

In this chapter:

- Who Needs Help?
- TGF2 Help
- Useful Web Sites
- Chapter Summary

Who Needs Help?

Who can you turn to if you are really stuck and you don't have a friend who can help with your problem? There are actually many resources, both within the product covered in this book and on the Internet, that you can use to help you make your games more quickly.

TGF2 Help

There are a number of ways of accessing help from within the program, and this should be your first point of call for getting support. Many problems you will face when you first start using a product will be fixed by using the product's built-in support features. Not only have you got the help you need at your fingertips, but you also won't need to wait a few hours or days to get a response from any online forums.

Help Files

All products have some form of Help file, be it an HTML document or a Microsoft Help formatted program. The good news is that TGF2 comes with an extensive Help facility.

To access the Help file, you will need to do the following:

1. Start TGF2 and go to the menu bar at the top of the program.

2. Select the Help option.

3. Select the Contents option. The Help system will now load.

The great thing about the Help system is that you can search for keywords and titles. This is very handy when you are looking for something specific.

Help About

The Help About is something that you will only use when contacting Clickteam's support staff or using their online forums. The Help About option displays information about the current program and the level of patches that are currently installed. Always mention the product and version number in any correspondence to ensure a faster response to your problem. The Help About option can be accessed from the menu system.

1. Start TGF2 and go to the menu bar at the top of the program.

2. Select the Help option.

3. Select the About the Games Factory 2 option. The About box will now load.

Tutorial

The Tutorial option (which can be accessed from the menu system, Help | Tutorial) loads a Help file that gives you an example game to create. If you are feeling like you need a bit more basic understanding of how to use the product, then the tutorial is a great way of improving your skills quickly and easily. First, take a look at how this tutorial is put together from the story and programming point of view.

You will learn a lot from looking at other games because it will help you understand the things that are required to make them interesting.

Examples

TGF2 comes with a number of game examples for you to try, which also allow you to explore the code in more detail. If you are stuck on a specific concept or game type, then take a look at the examples to see if that makes it easier for you to implement them in your own game. This is a very good way of finding out how a specific game type is made, but if you have problems, then copy the code bit by bit into a new game and see what it does.

Keyboard Shortcuts

Keyboard shortcuts allow you to use certain key combinations to do things more quickly, rather than finding items within the menu system. Within TGF2 there is a default set of shortcut commands, but you can also amend them to suit your own requirements. Over time you may find that you are duplicating certain menu combinations when you are developing your games. So by setting up your own keyboard shortcuts, you will be able to work more quickly and efficiently. Your other option is not to change the defaults but instead to make a list of all the important key combinations that you use for future reference.

To view the default keyboard preferences, do the following:

1. Start TGF2 and go to the menu bar at the top of the program.

2. Select the Tools option.

3. Select the Keyboard Shortcuts option.

Some default key combinations can be seen in Table 12.1.

Patches and Service Packs

You should always install the latest patches to make sure that if you are having problems, it's not something that has already been fixed in a later release. You will also find that people are more willing to help you with your problem if you have installed the most up-to-date version, as they will ask you to update before offering advice. Patches usually include fixes to bugs, but they also sometimes include new features, so it's to your benefit to keep current. If you are in the middle of the development of a game, you should consider waiting a few days or

Table 12.1 Common Key Combinations

Action	Key Combination	Details
Copy	Ctrl+C	Copy the selection and put it on the clipboard
Cut	Ctrl+X	Cut the selection and put it on the clipboard
Delete	Delete	Delete the selected object
Event Editor	Ctrl+E	Open Event Editor window
Frame Editor	Ctrl+M	Open Frame Editor window
Help	Shift+F1	Display help for clicked on buttons, menus, and windows
New	Ctrl+N	Create a new document
Open	Ctrl+O	Open an existing document
Paste	Ctrl+V	Insert clipboard contents
Play	F5	Play the current frame from the current position
Print	Ctrl+P	Print the active document
Redo	Ctrl+Y	Redo the previously undone action
Run Application	F8	Run the current application
Run Frame	F7	Run the current frame
Save	Ctrl+S	Save the active document
Select All	Ctrl+A	Select the entire document
Storyboard Editor	Ctrl+B	Open the Storyboard window
Undo	Ctrl+Z	Undo the last action
Zoom In	F2	Zoom the current window inwards
Zoom Out	F3	Zoom the current window outwards
Zoom to Fit	F4	Set the zoom factor of the current window to obtain a complete display

even a couple of weeks before applying a new patch. Though unlikely, it is possible that this could cause you problems with the program you are already working on, which could have catastrophic results. Before applying the patch, please make sure that you have already backed up any programs you're making so that it's possible to roll back to a previous release without losing any code.

Useful Web Sites

For information, the Internet is great, and if you are looking for product information and support, then the Internet will be your best friend. Not only can you find instant results to your problems, but also you will be able to locate helpful materials and downloads such as tutorials/game examples.

Here is a quick round-up of useful sites.

Game Creation for Teens

http://www.gamecreationforteens.co.uk

To accompany this book, a special Web site has been created to give you all the latest information and updates, including information on game creation.

Clickteam

http://www.clickteam.com

This is the home of TGF2 and its more powerful brother, Multimedia Fusion 2. From here, you can download demo versions of other products that you might need or read articles and information about the products. Please register for both the mailing list and the forums. This will mean that you can keep up-to-date on developments as they happen, but you also have the ability to post questions to any problems you get while you are making your games. Users on the forum are generally very efficient and helpful, which usually means you will get a response within 24 hours, if not sooner. As with all forums, it is best to read the FAQs before posting, as there are rules to be followed to ensure that things go according to plan.

Madword Arcade

http://www.madword.com

The Madword Arcade is a Web site that provides a set of games for people to play online. Many of the games on the site have been made with the Games Factory, so it's a good place to get some inspiration.

Clickconvention

http://www.clickconvention.com

Every year a group of dedicated developers get together and show what they have been working on. There have been five conventions so far, four near London in the UK and one in Paris, France. Users have traveled from all around the world to go to this user event, from countries such as Australia, the U.S., and parts of Europe. Check out the Web site for when the next event will happen and what is going to be shown. Clickteam staff and developers have also been present at these events, showing off their latest developments and product betas. You can find out what is in development and what exciting new products you might be using in the future. You will also get to meet like-minded individuals who are interested in making games at this event, so it's a great place to make new friends and even get people to help you answer those difficult development questions. If the event is too far for you to travel, then keep an eye on the Web site as information and photos of the event are posted there.

Retro Remakes

http://www.retroremakes.com

One of the most popular retro Web sites currently available is this Remakes site. Here, many game creators make remakes of old games for the PC platform and then upload them so that you can download and play. Retro Remakes also holds a yearly competition that brings in even more games to their database, but also means that you can enter to win thousands of dollars of prizes. All this from making a remake of an old game can't be bad, can it? It will depend on your age whether or not you recognize any of the games being mentioned, but it still is a very useful Web site if you want to get the look and feel of older "Retro" games.

Ovine by Design

http://www.ovine.net

A favorite Web site for people looking at re-creating old computer games is Ovine.net. Ovine is a small game-making team that designs games and remakes in their spare time. Visit this Web site to get some ideas.

eJay

http://www.ejay.com

Want to make your own music for your games, but don't have a musical bone in your body? What if you cannot play an instrument or you just don't know where to start? eJay is a very popular music creator, and best of all, the songs you create with it are royalty free. Containing around 4,000 royalty free samples, eJay lets you combine them to make musical scores using a simple, yet very effective, graphical interface. You can then save your masterpiece into a standard format, which you can import into TGF2. Although some of the tunes can sound very "samey," it does also allow you to download more samples or import your own so you can make them more unique.

Chapter Summary

There are many user sites available for TGF2, and you should take some time to search for them on the Internet and see which ones you like best. Not all sites will be to your taste and some may be at the wrong age group for you to want to read, but you never know when you might be surprised at what you can find. Make sure you take some time when you purchase any product to read the Help files and try out the tutorials so that you can get into making games more quickly. Above all—have fun making games.

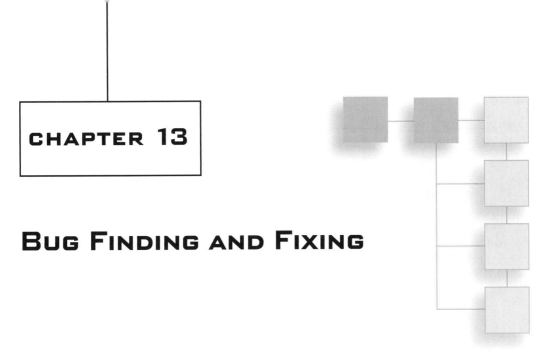

CHAPTER 13

Bug Finding and Fixing

In this chapter:

- What Are Bugs?

- Bug Fixing and Product Releases

- The Debugger

- Testing Run-Through

- Chapter Summary

In this chapter, we will be looking at program problems and bugs, how to find them, and then how to fix them. No matter how hard you try, bugs will appear in any program you write, but it is very important to ensure that you minimize them before you distribute your game. We will also be looking at ways that you can work out where a bug is within your program and remove it (not always as easy as it sounds). Finally, we will go through the tool that TGF2 has for giving you the best chance of squashing those nasty bugs—the Debugger.

What Are Bugs?

Computers, and the software used to run them, have been made by humans. Unfortunately, no matter how hard we try, we cannot seem to prevent problems with incorrect code or design issues from happening. These issues can cause random crashes and data corruption at any time, and they can be very infuriating for the user of the PC who is having the problem. You can also introduce bugs when you are programming and making games in TGF2 by having incorrect coding in the Event Editor. The key is making sure you look for the bugs and try to reduce them whenever possible.

Bug Fixing and Product Releases

There are a number of areas where you can fix bugs or ensure that all bugs have been removed. This process can be broken up into a number of phases, and although this is based on normal product releases, it's a good process for you to follow as well:

- **General Bug Fixing:** When you are creating your game, you should constantly test (and keep testing) to see if it works during the creation process. This testing is just to confirm that you have completed a particular section of code and can move on to the next part of the program. You may also find issues with the look and feel and general stability of the program. At this point, you are performing simple checks while making your game, because you will not be making any particular effort to find bugs right now.

- **Alpha Version:** When the product is in a suitable condition and a lot of the functionality has been implemented, you can then say your product is at version *Alpha*. This means that it is still unstable, but it is in a state where a lot of the options work (though not necessarily all), and it has the general look and feel of the final product. The product may still have some major bugs and issues with it, but this is the first version that is considered suitable enough to show people the work in progress (even if you are a beginning creator). The Alpha is used to get feedback on how the product sticks together and if the interface works well enough. This is the final stage of development before the product will be locked down with regard to features and its final look and feel. The end of the Alpha stage is an indication that this is the beginning of the final program and its functionality.

- **Beta:** At the end of the Alpha process, you will usually have comments back about how the product looks and if the interface works well. Once you are happy that you have taken the comments on board and have made final decisions about the interface (and have made those changes to the product), then you enter the Beta stage. The Beta stage is where the product is fully locked down with regard to functionality, look, and feel. This stage means all that needs to be done is removing any bugs within the program. You can give this version to your testers, who will then try and locate any problems within the game. Beta testers could be a group of friends, or anyone who has downloaded the game from your Web site and replies to you with comments.

- **Post Release:** After the product has been released, there will be people using the game on configurations that you may not have expected or ways that even the Beta testers didn't pick up. There are generally bugs to be fixed once the product is available to a larger number of people.

Testers

Beta testers are an essential resource for finding bugs within your games. Any game developer who has been working on a product for a while will find it harder to find bugs since he is so used to the product. A new user to the product tries things that the developer just wouldn't think about, so that person can be a great asset for finding those bugs you didn't even know about.

The Debugger

One of the new features of the latest release of TGF2 is the Debugger. This new functionality allows developers to search for program bugs within their games with much more ease. The Debugger is very much inline with code-based programming languages and offers lots of nice little features to make the developer's life much easier. Every program you make contains data information; for example, the current number of lives the player has and the location of the spaceship on the screen. All of this information is essential if you want to fix issues with your program. The new Debugger allows you to get access to all of these details so you can spend more time developing your programs, rather than bug finding.

Starting the Debugger

To make the Debugger start, you will need to have a program running within TGF2. Once you have opened up one of your games, if you run the frame or the

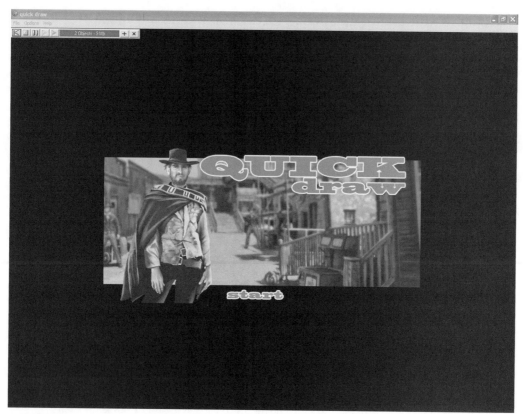

Figure 13.1
The Debugger open and ready to use.

Figure 13.2
A close-up of the Debugger bar.

whole game, then the Debugger will appear in the top left-hand corner, as shown in Figure 13.1.

If you look at Figure 13.2, this is a closer look at what the Debugger bar contains.

There are a number of buttons and functionality that you can access:

■ If you click the + icon on the right-hand side of the Debugger bar, it will expand the amount of information that you will be able to see. All options and program data can now be viewed. Within the whole program (each frame, object, and so on) is specific information, be it location on

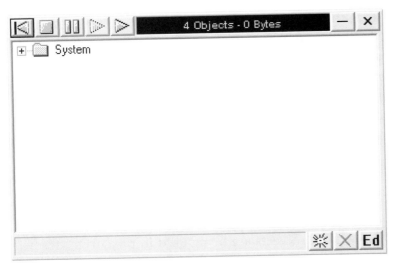

Figure 13.3
The Debugger expanded to reveal more information.

the screen, screen size, current counter values, or string details. The expanded Debugger can be seen in Figure 13.3. To collapse it back, you need to click the minus sign that replaced the plus sign when you clicked expand.

- The first button on the Debugger bar is called the Rewind button (the line with the left-pointing arrow), and it signifies that the program will start from the beginning of the frame once clicked. This is very useful if you are trying to track a bug and want to watch what is being changed (something we will detail shortly). You can keep repeating the process until you have found the problem.

  There is an example of how the Go to Start of Frame button works on the CD-ROM. The example is called debugger1 and it is located in the Debugger folder; open this file up in TGF2 to see how it works.

- The square icon on the Debugger bar is the Stop button. This stops the frame and program from running, and it will also close the running game and the Debugger.

- The third icon is the Pause button, which will pause your program (meaning that nothing will happen on the games playfield) until you press Play to start it back up. This will allow you to get to a specific point in the program and then check the result of the current data being stored by TGF2.

- The fourth icon from the left looks like a grayed-out right-pointing arrow, and it's called the Next Step button. It allows you to step through your game code a line at a time. To use this function, you will need to pause the program first by using the Pause button mentioned previously. This is a very useful option if you want to slowly see what changes are made to your program (as things can happen very quickly otherwise, and you might miss something).

- The fifth icon is the Play button. Once you have paused the program, you will use this to start it back at real time (playing at normal speed).

- The display in the middle of the Debugger bar shows two bits of useful information: first, how many objects are being used in the current frame, and second, the amount of bytes for the total memory used by the application.

The default information that is shown within the expanded Debugger is for the basic application level. What this means is that if you created a blank game, this information would always be present (top-level details are separate from anything you might add, such as game objects you might have placed in your game). To see what information is contained within the expanded Debugger box, see Figure 13.4.

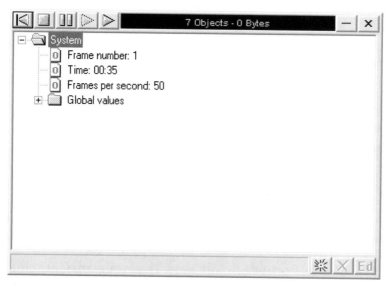

Figure 13.4
Basic information that is stored in the Debugger.

Expanding the System folder will give you all the standard game information. Frame Number refers to the current frame that is running within the game. The Time is the actual time that frame has been running for (very important to remember that the time is reset between frames). You also have another expandable folder, which allows you to see all of the global values being used within the program. At the bottom of the expanded Debugger, you will also see three additional buttons that you can use to add and remove additional items. The first icon is to add additional items, the second is to delete any items, and finally you will have an "Ed" button, which is used when you want to edit specific data entries.

Running Time

Although the time in each frame is reset in the System folder, when you move to another frame, you could create an object that saves the total running time for the application. You could then add this information to the Debugger and view it.

Adding Items to the Debugger

You now want to add an item to the Debugger so that you can watch it and see what happens to it when your game is running. Open up the file called *debugadd*, which is located on the CD-ROM under the folder \debugger.

- Run the game by pressing the Run Application button on the toolbar. This will start the game and open the Debugger. Click the Start Game button within the game to move to frame 2.

- Click the Add Object to Debugger button, which will open up the dialogue box. Expand the Other Objects folder to reveal what objects you will need to add so that you can watch it. An example of this dialog is shown in Figure 13.5.

- We want to watch the score and the number of lives and see how they change when playing the game. Click the Score object and click OK. You will then need to add the score by using the same process.

- Begin to play the game, and you will notice that the score changes every time you hit a block, and the number of live objects will also be reduced every time the ball goes out of the play area on the right-hand side of the screen.

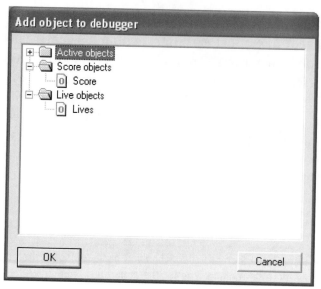

Figure 13.5
Click the + signs to see what you can add to the Debugger.

Objects in the Debugger

It is important to note that for each frame, you will need to set up your objects that you want to watch. Once you move frames, the Debugger resets the items within its list to just System. This is because each frame will have different objects allocated to it, so it needs to do this to refresh the list.

Testing Run-Through

To ensure that you fully understand the Debugger and the power that it has, below is a short run-through of a program that doesn't have a bug, but some configuration of the program has not been implemented. Hopefully, this will allow you to see what a great feature the Debugger is and how it can fix not only bugs in your code but also code that you may have forgotten to implement.

1. Start TGF2.

2. Click the menu option File and then Open to load a TGF2 file into the program.

3. Browse the CD-ROM for the Debugger folder (on the root of the CD) and locate a file called debugtest; double-click it so that it is loaded into TGF2.

4. Click the Run Application to make TGF2 start the game with the Debugger.

5. Click the plus sign on the Debugger bar to expand the view. Click the game's Start Game text, which will take you to the second frame where the game will start.

6. If you expand the System option within the Debugger, you will now see that the game is on frame 2, the time is incrementing upwards, and the frames-per-second value is changing rapidly. This shows that the game is currently running, and within the code, it is waiting for a key press to launch the ball.

7. Click the Pause button within the Debugger bar to pause the program. This will mean that you cannot make the ball move, as the code has effectively stopped running until you press Play again.

8. Click the Add Object to Debugger button to bring up the dialog box. You will see a dialog box with three items, called Active object, Score object, and Lives object. Expand the Score object. After you have done this, then highlight the Score object and click OK. Click the Add button again and do the same for the Lives object (expand the Live object option, highlight Lives, and then click OK).

9. You will immediately notice that the score is at 0, which is not a problem, as the game hasn't started yet. The player hasn't begun to destroy any of the blocks on the playfield, so he wouldn't have gained any score yet. You may also notice that the Lives object is currently set at 0. This would be set at the start of the game to whatever number is appropriate for your game. In the loaded game (the debugtest.mfa), the number of lives starts at 3. If you were to play the game and the bat missed the ball, you would find that you don't lose a life (as you don't have any anyway), and you would also notice that the Lives graphic doesn't show up on the game screen.

10. We can see this is a problem. The great thing about the Debugger is that you can actually edit the data while the game is paused. This allows you to test the game with different data results without needing to come out, reprogram, and then start the debugging process again. Click the Number of Lives object on the Debugger dialog box, and you will now see that the Ed button is no longer grayed out.

11. Click the Ed button, which will bring up the Edit dialogue box. Type in the number **3,** because this is what you want as the starting lives that the player begins with.

12. Immediately, the program is updated with the new results, and you will now notice that the Number of Lives graphic has three little circles in it (which represent each life).

13. If you now start the game and try to lose a life, you will see that it plays correctly, so you will need to close the game and Debugger and add the number of lives in the Initial # of Lives to 3 (this is located in the Runtime options, Properties tab).

Although this is a very simple example of a problem in your game, hopefully, it has proven how powerful, yet easy to use, the Debugger can be for the developer. You can now, in one screen, look for a bug, see if you can rectify it, and monitor the results.

Chapter Summary

Although bug fixing may be one of the last things that you do in the development of your game (and one of the last things on your mind), its importance shouldn't be understated. Fixing problems before releasing your games will ensure you don't get people emailing you and complaining when something doesn't work correctly.

INDEX

About the CD-ROM

The companion CD-ROM contains everything you will need to make all of the programs that are included in this book.

General Minimum System Requirements

You will need a computer that can run Windows 95 or better with a CD-ROM drive, a sound card, and a mouse.

Games Factory 2.0

(www.clickteam.com) Trial

The file name for the program is TGF2Demo.exe and is located in the Demos folder.

Minimum Requirements

- Operating system: Windows 95 with IE 4.0, Windows 98, Windows NT 4.0 with service pack 3 or above, Windows 2000, Windows XP, Windows Vista
- Pentium processor
- 32MB RAM with Windows 9x, 64MB with Windows NT, 128MB with 2000 and Windows XP, 512MB with Vista
- CD-ROM drive
- Graphics card with 8MB RAM or more (or minimum OS requirements)
- Sound card (optional, but recommended)
- 50–100MB free hard disk space

Recommended Requirements

- Operating system: Windows 98, Windows 2000, Windows XP, Windows Vista
- Pentium 4 processor
- 64MB RAM with Windows 98, 256MB RAM with Windows 2000 or XP, and 1GB RAM with Windows Vista
- CD-ROM drive
- Graphics card with 32MB RAM
- Sound card
- 200–500MB free hard disk space

Folders

A number of folders on the CD-ROM contain important files for use within this book, as well as useful information.

- **Debugger:** Files for Chapter 13.
- **Demos:** Location of the demo files that you can install.
- **Figures:** In the Figures folder on the CD-ROM, you will find color versions of every figure seen in the book.
- **TGFFILES:** Example file required for the animation chapter.
- **Games:** A selection of games to play that are made with TGF2.
- **Game1:** Files for Game 1
- **Game2:** Files for Game 2
- **Game3:** Files for Game 3